PUZZLES
AND BRAIN
TEASERS

Sudoku Puzzles, Word Games, Visual Challenges, and Tests of Logic

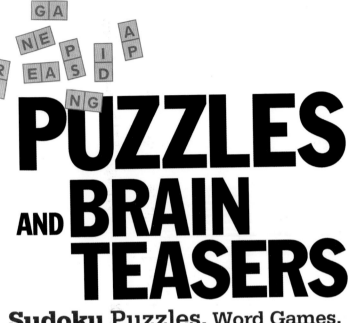

Reader's Digest

The Reader's Digest Association, Inc.
Pleasantville, NY / Montreal

ISBN 13: 978-0-7621-0848-0
ISBN 10: 0-7621-0848-7

Reader's Digest Pocket Guide: Puzzles and Brain Teasers was previously published as *Better Brain Power* (ISBN: 0-7621-0544-5).

PROJECT STAFF
Puzzle Editor **Robert Ronald**
Editor **Neil Wertheimer**
Creative Director **Michele Laseau**
Copy Editor **Jeanette Gingold**
Manufacturing Manager **John L. Cassidy**

All puzzles except the Sudoku and Kakuro puzzles commissioned and produced by Librios Publishing, London

Sudoku and Kakuro puzzles commissioned and produced by Inertia Software

Address any comments to:
        The Reader's Digest Association, Inc.
        Adult Trade Publishing
        Reader's Digest Road
        Pleasantville, NY 10570-7000

For more Reader's Digest products and information, visit our website: **rd.com**

Printed in China

1 3 5 7 9 10 8 6 4 2

Introduction
The Secret to Better Brain Power 4

Introduction

The Secret to Better Brain Power

It's no secret that some puzzles began as mere games and others as tools of learning. The best puzzles are both.

Puzzles also tap into the three elements of intelligence: analytical, creative, and practical (the puzzles in this book stretch all of them). Selected not only for their challenging nature, but also for their fun, this pocket guide is packed with enough puzzles to provide hours of stimulating and enriching mind play, at home or on the go.

Improve your language skills with our collection of riddles, magic squares, and other word puzzles. These brain bogglers will stretch your vocabulary and test your logic with stress-free games. No longer will your crossword remain unsolved! Your memory and visualization will get a boost from the section of visual puzzles, including classic matching and spot-the-difference games, while your everyday quantitative skills will be bolstered by our fun collection of number challenges.

The last section features Sudoku and Kakuro puzzles, some of the newest and most popular logic games. You may have merely spotted them in your local newspaper, attempted a few puzzles yourself, or you may be a dedicated enthusiast. Whatever your skill level, this book has a puzzle for you.

How does your brain react to a challenge: Can you see the patterns in shapes, words, and sequences? The answers are at the back of the book, but resist the temptation to turn to them before you tackle a puzzle. The solutions are easy to find, and most include explanations, but they are also lurking at the back of your mind. Look for them there, and have fun.

Word Puzzles

1

Can you work your way to the center of the grid starting from the top left? Words overlap, with the last one or two letters of each answer starting the next word. A few letters have been placed on the grid to keep you on the right track.

CLUES

1 Holy building (6)

2 Dairy product (6)

3 Not often (6)

4 Final Greek letter (5)

5 Old sailing ship (7)

6 Formerly (4)

7 In the middle (7)

8 Authorize (5)

9 Proprietor (5)

10 Rub out (5)

11 Group of words (8)

12 Sure (7)

13 Hidden (9)

14 Head man (6)

15 Mission (6)

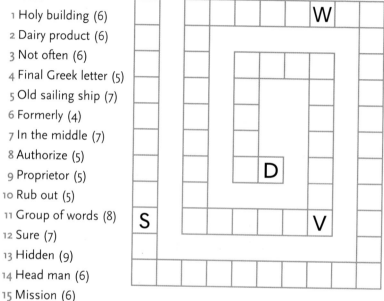

2 Use the letters in the shaded squares to find the name of a South American country.

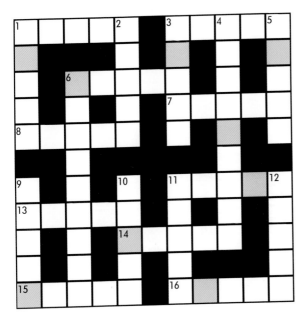

ACROSS

1 Assorted (5)

3 Deadly (5)

6 Short prayer (5)

7 Quota (5)

8 Prepared (5)

11 Pile (5)

13 Eye-cover (5)

14 Surplus (5)

15 Walk (5)

16 Dangerous (5)

DOWN

1 Army rank (5)

2 Journal (5)

3 New (5)

4 Large hairy spider (9)

5 Powerful light (5)

6 Thanks (9)

9 Divide (5)

10 In front (5)

11 Engine (5)

12 Unclean (5)

3

Can you unravel the anagrams in the clues to fill in the grid and complete this mixed-up crossword?

ACROSS

1 Rice beds (8)

7 Or Len (5)

8 Hated (5)

9 See rum (6)

10 Bare (4)

12 Peat (4)

14 Specie (6)

17 Aides (5)

18 Idles (5)

19 Steep dam (8)

DOWN

1 "D" star (5)

2 Lemons (6)

3 Dire (4)

4 Caber (5)

5 Late throb (9)

6 Shot crier (9)

11 Suites (6)

13 Inapt (5)

15 Raced (5)

16 Meat (4)

4

All the black squares in this symmetrical grid have been replaced with letters. Can you discover where the black squares should lie and color them in? Number the squares as you go, then enter the correct numbers against the jumbled list of clues.

ACROSS

Remain
Large house
Tug
Phobia
Plenty
School group
Insect
Finished
First appearance
Noisy
Shortly
Animal skin
Stadium

E	R	I	C	L	A	S	S	U	R	E
P	U	L	L	E	Y	C	L	O	U	D
O	S	S	A	M	P	L	E	I	I	G
S	T	A	Y	U	A	N	D	O	N	E
T	I	D	E	A	S	T	H	U	S	R
O	R	M	A	N	S	I	O	N	C	E
R	K	I	S	S	A	P	U	C	E	C
M	O	T	H	U	G	E	P	E	L	T
O	P	T	A	R	E	N	A	B	O	U
F	E	A	R	G	E	T	S	O	O	N
F	N	U	D	E	B	U	T	A	K	E

DOWN

Corrosion
Stiff mud
Glance
Beyond
Snow vehicle
Wreck

Difficult
Sea journey
Undo
Small weight
Allow in
Tempest
Build

5 To get you in the cryptic mood this crossword has standard Down clues but cryptic Across clues.

ACROSS

1 Not all those who give birth rest (6)

4 Degas almost looked back and grew older (4)

8 Pen account back to ship's room (5)

9 Lunatic adores no Eastern routes (5)

10 Bought it in crashed–up mess (9)

11 Become friendly with a colleague (9)

14 Circle an electric wire for a Mediterranean fruit (5)

15 Some axe the renal anaesthetic (5)

16 Sing about the indicator (4)

17 Made a lord on close inspection? (6)

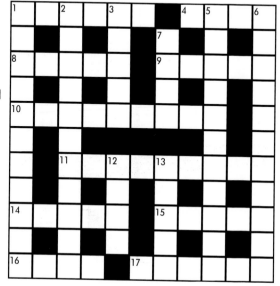

DOWN

1 Jobs (11)

2 Sleeping during winter (11)

3 A tract of land for raising cattle (5)

5 The male parent of your parent (11)

6 Became invisible (11)

7 Prepares for a military confrontation (4)

12 Spies (4)

13 Small, thin pancake (5)

6 Use the letters in the shaded squares to find the name of a famous writer.

ACROSS

1 Groove (4)
3 Profit (4)
5 Increase (5)
6 Stardom (4)
8 Emphasis (6)
10 Spaceman (9)
13 Obstacle (6)
15 Run off (4)
16 Sea map (5)
17 Assignment (4)
18 Simple (4)

DOWN

1 Rigid (5)
2 Genuine (4)
3 Equipment (4)
4 Hospital worker (5)
7 Skinflint (5)
8 Incline (5)
9 Identical (5)
11 Flour grain (5)
12 Trivial (5)
14 Ship's floor (4)
15 Destiny (4)

7 Can you work your way to the center of the grid? Words overlap, with the last one or two letters of each answer starting the next word. A few letters have been inserted on the grid to help you out.

CLUES

1 Damaged (6)

2 Sufficient (6)

3 Phantom (5)

4 Possible chess ending (9)

5 Awful (8)

6 Tuition periods (6)

7 Beginning (5)

8 Everlasting (7)

9 Sacrificial table (5)

10 Turn up (6)

11 Snake poison (5)

12 Left out (7)

13 Teach (7)

14 Cooking measure (8)

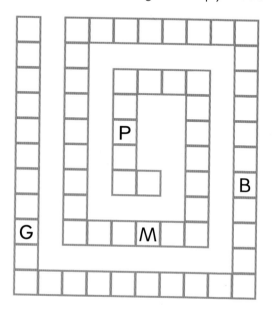

8 Use the context of each sentence to work out the missing word for the grid.

ACROSS

7 Please be more _____—I need your help (11)

8 The ____ of a church usually contains the altar (4)

9 I go to hear the priest's _____ each Sunday (6)

10 There seems to be a lot of _____ on this telephone line (9)

13 A _____ carries your golf clubs (6)

15 ____ is the largest of the continents (4)

17 My gums hurt because my last _____ is about to come through (6,5)

DOWN

1 The car broke down so often I sold it for _____ (5)

2 I won't eat roast beef without _____(11)

3 That rooster courts a new ____ daily (3)

4 I can tell it's a picture of a saint because of the ____ around his head (4)

5 I don't want to _____ you, but real magic doesn't exist (11)

6 Agriculture dominates the economy of _____, particularly the growing of tea and coffee (5)

9 Marry in _____ and repent at leisure (5)

11 Don't _____ or your face will stay like that (5)

12 I like hunky men who are ____ (5)

14 Marilyn Monroe was a 1960's ____ (4)

16 This is the pilot speaking: our ____ is 08:15 hours (1.1.1.)

9

Can you work your way to the center of the grid? Words overlap by one or two letters. A few letters have been inserted to keep you on the right track.

CLUES

1 Objection (7)

2 Unusual (7)

3 Sign of the zodiac (6)

4 Catch fire (6)

5 Schoolmaster (7)

6 Decrease (6)

7 Breakfast food (6)

8 Frighten (5)

9 Enigma (7)

10 Racing boat (5)

11 Unrest (7)

12 In front (7)

13 Liquid measure (6)

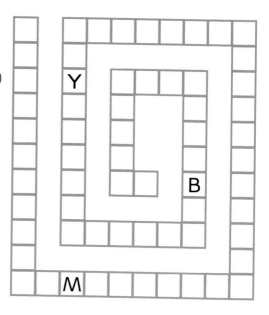

10 All the black squares in this symmetrical grid have been replaced with letters. Can you discover where the black squares should lie and color them in? Number the squares for the Across and Down words, and finally enter the correct numbers against the jumbled list of clues.

ACROSS

Infant
Between
Fortunate
Seashore
Join
Twelve
Clutch
Winch
Weary
Weighty

DOWN

Roman vehicle
Turn red
Taint
Soiled
Welcome
Christmas song
Hunting dog
Beg
Convenient
Teach

B	E	A	C	H	O	G	R	A	S	P
L	O	R	I	A	R	R	I	V	A	L
U	N	C	O	N	N	E	C	T	O	E
S	O	H	E	D	Y	E	K	A	T	A
H	E	A	V	Y	E	T	I	R	E	D
S	U	R	F	E	D	A	R	N	N	A
C	H	I	L	D	A	H	O	I	S	T
A	P	O	E	I	C	O	N	S	E	R
R	A	T	H	R	O	U	G	H	L	A
O	D	I	N	T	E	N	D	E	L	I
L	U	C	K	Y	S	D	O	Z	E	N

11

Use the letters in the shaded squares to find the name of a popular Christmas song.

ACROSS

1 Male voice (5)
3 Inferior to (5)
6 Serenity (5)
7 Think alike (5)
8 Phantom (5)
11 Commence (5)
13 Be good at (5)
14 Subside (5)
15 Enticed (5)
16 Religious belief (5)

DOWN

1 Leather strap (5)
2 Oven cook (5)
3 Baker's product (5)
4 Oil (9)
5 Irrigate (5)
6 Film equipment (9)
9 Mutineer (5)
10 Tasteless (5)
11 Workforce (5)
12 Strong (5)

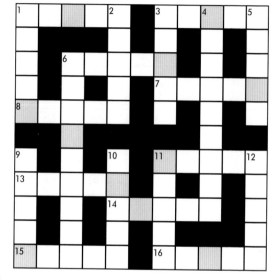

12 The Across clues are cryptic but the Down clues are standard in this puzzle.

ACROSS

1 Yearn like a Guevara (4)

3 Sounds like I could buy a Focus (6)

7 Owing to fatal illness (5,6)

9 Understand course admitted to my size anyhow (10)

11 Resonant? It's ludi-crously loud! (10)

13 Tried for undermining the government by being too tall, reportedly (4,7)

14 Give testimony for first April, exam comes after end of August (6)

15 Exclusive tour around Lyon (4)

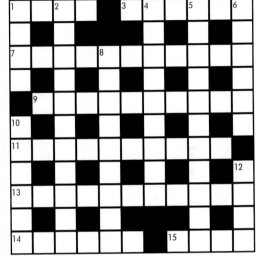

DOWN

1 Someone who acts as assistant (4)

2 Muhammad Ali was one (11)

4 Tall plant which gives edible produce (5,4)

5 An evil inherited by all descendants of Adam (8,3)

6 One of Santa's reindeer (6)

8 Viral inflammation of the liver (9)

10 Respiratory disorder (6)

12 Covetousness (4)

13

Can you work your way to the center of the grid? Words overlap, with the last one or two letters of each answer starting the next word. Two letters have been placed on the grid to keep you on the right track.

CLUES

1 Gruesome (7)

2 Stay behind (6)

3 Lowest point (5)

4 Sturdy (6)

5 Staying power (7)

6 Lineage (8)

7 Give way (5)

8 Take apart (9)

9 Deadly (6)

10 Height (8)

11 Grow (6)

12 Peril (6)

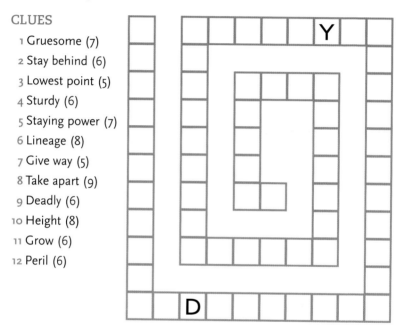

14 Another mixed-up crossword! Can you unravel these anagrams to find the solutions?

ACROSS

1 Alien item (9)

6 Was Dr (5)

7 Cruet (5)

9 Tice (4)

10 Cot rod (6)

12 Tin emu (6)

14 Hags (4)

17 Alert (5)

18 Point (5)

19 Ravers day (9)

DOWN

2 Steal (5)

3 Sham (4)

4 On a tin (6)

5 Strut (5)

6 Claimed (7)

8 Hare net (7)

11 Averts (6)

13 To end (5)

15 Sitar (5)

16 Stop (4)

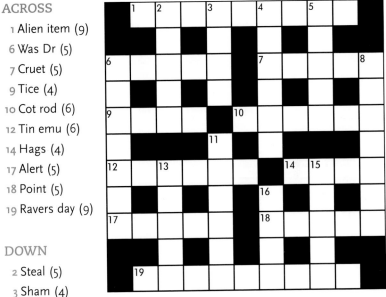

15 A moderately tough fill-in-the-blanks crossword.

ACROSS

4 The seven bright stars of Ursa Major are also known as the ___ _____(3,6)

7 Make yourself useful and _____ that cream for me (4)

8 I'm going to let my unused gym membership _____ (6)

9 Don't be so _____—can you do any better? (5)

10 That bee might _____ you (5)

12 I can take a joke, but I'm tired of being his _____ (6)

13 My favorite Muppets character was the Swedish ____ (4)

14 The Jolly Green Giant advertises _____ (9)

DOWN

1 The _____ was a stadium for horse races (10)

2 Don't grasp that cow's ____ too tightly! (5)

3 Hey, don't shoot the _____! (9)

5 _____ covers shaping, modeling, carving and sculpture (7,3)

6 Most cities have a _____ area with Asian influences (9)

11 The score is 40 all—_____! (5)

16 Which word, when tagged onto the first word, will form another word, and when placed in front of the second word will also form another word?

page (......................) hem

17 Find the word in this strange anagram.

Not bay?

18 Which is the odd word out and why?

Schmaltzy   Yachtsmen   Brainwave

Feudalism   Sparkling   Lethargic

19 Just one set of the following letters is an anagram of a five-letter word. Can you discover which it is?

RHUED   YRFOM   MECUN

GEROC   KERCA   FEBLO

20

Answer the clues to find eight answers. These letters can then be transferred into the main grid to give you a comical quotation and the name of the comic to whom it is attributed.

1D	2B	3A	4G	5C	6D	■	7G	8E	9C
■	10F	11C	12D	13C	■	14G	15F	■	16E
17C	■	18F	19E	20G	21H	22A	■	23B	24H
25G	■	26E	27G	28A	29H	30H	31B	32D	■
33G	34B	35H	36G	37F	38H	39F	■	40D	41H
42H	43E	■							

A Recently stolen or smuggled

$\overline{}\ \overline{}\ \overline{}$
22 28 3

B Engage for work

$\overline{}\ \overline{}\ \overline{}\ \overline{}$
23 2 34 31

C Shabby and untidy

$\overline{}\ \overline{}\ \overline{}\ \overline{}\ \overline{}$
9 11 5 13 17

D A cherished desire

$\overline{}\ \overline{}\ \overline{}\ \overline{}\ \overline{}$
32 6 1 12 40

E Exercises evaluating knowledge

$\overline{}\ \overline{}\ \overline{}\ \overline{}\ \overline{}$
8 43 19 16 26

F A throng or clique

$\overline{}\ \overline{}\ \overline{}\ \overline{}\ \overline{}$
37 15 39 18 10

G Opinions that are worth a penny?

$\overline{}\ \overline{}\ \overline{}\ \overline{}\ \overline{}\ \overline{}\ \overline{}\ \overline{}$
20 7 14 36 33 4 27 25

H Final path of an aircraft while landing

$\overline{}\ \overline{}\ \overline{}\ \overline{}\ \overline{}\ \overline{}\ \overline{}\ \overline{}$
41 29 30 42 35 24 21 38

21 For this wordfinder puzzle, you must find words of three letters or more by traveling horizontally, vertically or diagonally to adjacent letters. Each letter may be used once only in each new word. Plurals and well-known proper names are allowed.

----

22 The dice blocks each have a six-letter word written on them, but unfortunately you can see only three sides. When you have solved the clues, the first column will reveal a ten-letter word.

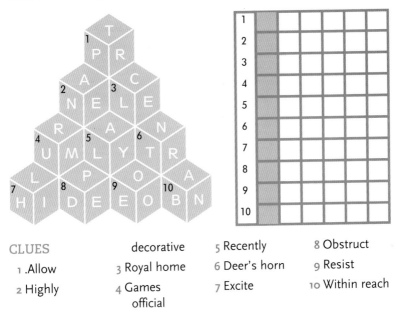

CLUES

decorative

1. Allow

2. Highly

3. Royal home

4. Games official

5. Recently

6. Deer's horn

7. Excite

8. Obstruct

9. Resist

10. Within reach

23 Place all the words listed on the next page into the grid. Will they fit? If you do it right, they will.

3-LETTER WORDS	ERROR	7-LETTER WORDS	9-LETTER WORDS
AIR	GROWN	CHOKING	CUSTOMERS
INK	IDEAS	COWBOYS	HURRICANE
INN	NAMES	ENTERED	INCORRECT
SIR	OILED	HARNESS	REPLACING
5-LETTER WORDS	OLDER	RESTORE	SPIRITUAL
	OPERA	SHRINKS	UNCOVERED
CHOIR	RACES	SPONGES	WELL-KNOWN
CLAPS	RADIO	WEIGHTS	WINDMILLS
DEPTH	REINS		
DRIVE	SAVED		
	STAIR		

24 Test your vocabulary with this verbal teaser. We've provided four definitions—but only one is correct. The others are designed to confuse you.

Tureen

Tall building   Large dish

Small coin   Pointed beard

----

25 What is the opposite of meteoric?

Transient   Meticulous   Mellow   Steady   Esoteric

----

26 Change WARM into COLD by altering one letter at a time.

WARM

✎ - - - - - - - - - - - - - - - - - District

- - - - - - - - - - - - - - - - - Joker

- - - - - - - - - - - - - - - - - Twine

COLD

27 Which word is hidden in this anagram?

Be loud

✎ -

28 Solve the clues provided to complete the pyramid. When you've done that, the 14 letters in the pyramid can be arranged to make a single word (clue: movie art).

CLUES

1 Belonging to me

2 Food with a crust

3 Suspend

4 Thespian

✎ -

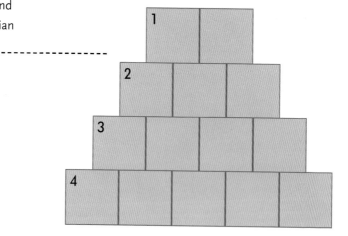

29 Place all the pieces into the grid so that a valid crossword is formed. Remember that crossword grids possess half-turn symmetry. The colored blocks will also help.

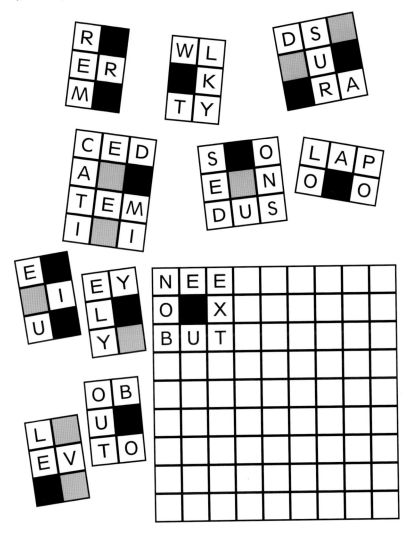

30 In this alphabetical quiz, we take you through an A to Z of answers, each of which has all but one letter missing. How many can you reconstruct?

Scientific equipment	A __ __ A __ A __ __ __
Blown spheres	B __ B B __ __ __
It preys on your mind	C __ __ __ C __ __ __ C __
United we stand, ___ we fall	D __ __ __ D __ D
St. _____, U.S. hospital drama	E __ __ E __ __ E __ E
The golden anniversary	F __ F __ __ __ __ __
Swimmers wear them	G __ G G __ __ __
A vital statistic	H __ __ __ H __
Type of police parade	I __ __ __ __ I __ I __ __ __ I __ __
A feeling of envy	J __ __ __ __ __ __ __
Rap with the knuckles	K __ __ __ K
Without exaggeration	L __ __ __ __ __ L L __
Embalmed body	M __ M M __
A golfer's favorite hole	N __ N __ __ __ __ N __ __
The other side	O __ __ O __ __ __ __ O __
Marionette	P __ P P __ __
In a line, like its five vowels	Q __ __ __ __ __ __
Store of water	R __ __ __ R __ __ __ R
Don't run with them	S __ __ S S __ __ S
You go to a doctor for it	T __ __ __ T __ __ __ T
That's odd	U __ U __ U __ __
Clear in the memory	V __ V __ __
Native American dwelling	W __ __ W __ __
Charles Foster Kane's home	X __ __ __ __ __
The day before	Y __ __ __ __ __ __ __ Y
Jagged line	Z __ __ Z __ __

31 Can you spot the following musical terms and instruments in the grid? They may be found across, down or diagonally in any direction.

Q	I	K	W	A	E	B	N	Z	I	T	H	E	R
E	M	F	G	C	N	J	T	C	P	S	P	V	A
L	W	T	R	I	F	L	E	K	Y	U	Z	D	T
G	X	V	S	H	A	L	L	O	W	L	U	R	I
U	Y	P	J	W	L	K	U	N	U	F	C	B	U
B	A	N	J	O	E	W	A	T	C	H	X	H	G
Q	O	R	K	Y	N	V	E	U	E	N	P	R	A
D	E	O	W	P	R	A	H	S	T	E	A	D	Y
K	Q	H	V	L	N	F	I	I	U	B	W	J	L
E	Z	Y	U	T	R	U	M	P	E	T	H	G	L
W	A	J	I	K	L	U	N	I	A	Z	E	Q	A
S	T	A	R	S	R	U	L	P	N	T	P	A	R
A	V	L	A	D	O	C	L	E	F	I	C	B	G
E	N	T	E	R	T	A	I	N	T	E	M	P	O

BANJO	FLUTE	MINIM
BUGLE	GUITAR	PIANO
CELLO	HARP	PIPE
CLEF	HORN	TEMPO
CODA	LARGO	WALTZ
DRUM	LUTE	ZITHER

32 A letter-fit puzzle with a twist. Every word listed at the top of the opposite page is five letters long, so what goes where? That's for you to work out. (We've placed one word on the grid to get you started.)

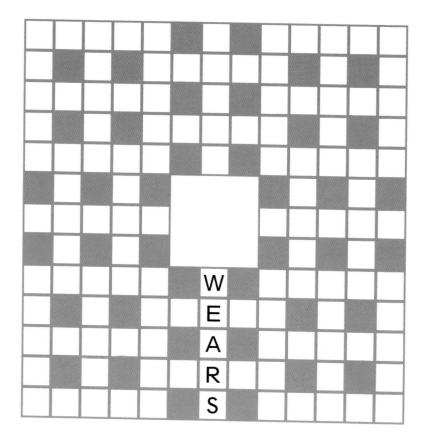

AGAIN	ENEMY	OTHER	TIDAL
AGING	FABLE	RANGE	TOWEL
ANGER	GATES	RAZOR	TREAT
APRON	GLIDE	REEDS	URGED
DENSE	GREAT	REFER	USING
DISKS	GREEN	RHYME	~~WEARS~~
DRAMA	IDEAS	ROADS	WHEAT
EIGHT	ITEMS	STEER	WIPED
EMPTY	LOYAL	SUGAR	ZEBRA

33 Just one of the sets of letters below is an anagram of a five-letter word. Find the word.

LUBRA   OPRDA   UGRNA   NETDR   HEDCN

✎ --

34 Answers in this word square read the same across as down.

CLUES

1 We need to ___ the bathroom walls
2 The ___ is part of the eye
3 The man walked with a ___
4 You can ___ a ship on the horizon

1	2	3	4
2			
3			
4			

35 Change NEED to WANT by solving three clues. One letter only is altered at each step.

NEED

✎ - - - - - - - - - - - - - - - - **Useless plant**

- - - - - - - - - - - - - - - - - - **Make way**

- - - - - - - - - - - - - - - - - - **Magician's stick**

WANT

36 Solve the clues provided to fill out the word pyramid. When the pyramid is complete, the 15 letters can be arranged into one word (clue: something mathematical).

CLUES

1 The Roman numeral for 1000 (1)

2 Expression of refusal (2)

3 Spasmodic twitching of muscles (3)

4 Group of three (4)

5 Big (5)

✎ -

37 Can you spot the following capital cities in the grid?
They may be found across, down or diagonally in any direction.

A	N	A	V	A	H	T	S	G	H	E	N	O	W
T	O	R	O	N	T	O	B	V	I	E	N	N	A
Q	B	T	S	F	D	C	G	N	M	P	J	M	R
O	S	U	T	Q	P	Z	R	T	O	O	I	L	S
Y	I	L	P	A	K	W	E	X	T	L	M	H	A
U	L	P	R	E	W	B	C	R	I	Z	S	L	W
R	O	I	A	N	I	A	N	S	O	T	K	O	U
K	S	T	Y	V	I	X	M	J	G	M	C	N	Y
D	A	S	L	R	A	L	L	W	U	S	E	D	C
U	E	S	O	F	I	A	D	R	O	A	J	O	S
B	L	L	V	W	Q	R	A	M	Y	T	U	N	E
L	B	U	S	R	L	U	B	A	K	W	I	J	L
I	T	E	W	D	S	B	L	A	O	S	W	U	K
N	A	I	R	O	B	I	A	N	T	P	L	I	Q

CAIRO	LISBON	OTTAWA	TOKYO
DUBLIN	LONDON	PARIS	VIENNA
HAVANA	MOSCOW	QUITO	WARSAW
KABUL	NAIROBI	ROME	
LIMA	OSLO	SOFIA	

38 What does that word mean? We've provided four definitions—but only one is correct. The other three are designed to confuse you.

ENDEAVOR

Consume   Confusion

Conclusion   Attempt

39 Which word, when tagged onto the first word, will form another word, and when placed in front of the second word will form another word?

bar (_____) say

40

Can you squeeze these words into the grid? One has been positioned to get you started.

						R				
						E				
						E				
						D				

4-LETTER WORDS

DADO
DUST
EYES
HOOP
~~REED~~
SIDE
STAY
ZERO

6-LETTER WORDS

CLASPS
DISMAY
GALLOP
GENTLE
GRAINS
GRASSY
OXYGEN
PAPERS
POETRY
RAGGED
REPEAT
SENSES
SPEARS
SYMBOL

TRIBES
YEARLY

7-LETTER WORDS

ABILITY
ACROBAT

ALARMED
EARLIER
ECONOMY
EMPEROR
ENABLED
GERMANY

LUNCHES
OUTLINE
PUNCHES
SCENERY
SPECIAL
TEARING

41 Test your vocabulary with this verbal teaser. We've provided four definitions, but only one is correct. Can you spot it?

NOUGAT

Confectionery   Turkish

Toothache   Dignitary

Zero

---

42 Solve the clues, adding a letter at a time, and complete the pyramid.

CLUES

Neuter pronoun (2)   __ __

Small unit (3)   __ __ __

Wound (4)   __ __ __ __

Snapper (5)   __ __ __ __ __

Sharp to the taste (6)   __ __ __ __ __ __

Bird (7)   __ __ __ __ __ __ __

43 Which of these is the correct definition of the word at the top?

TORPID

Very hot

Frightening

Bullfighter

Sluggish

----

44 Find the word that links the pair of words below.

back (.......) some

45 Can you find the six-letter word contained in this anagram?

air sob

----

46 In this wordfinder puzzle, try to find words of three letters or more by traveling horizontally, vertically or diagonally to adjacent letters. Each letter may be used only once in each new word. Plurals and well-known proper names are allowed.

S	N	O
P	I	C
M	A	H

----

47 Just one of the sets of letters below is an anagram of a six-letter English word. Can you find the word?

HURCOL

LEACBN

LERDCA

YRCOLT

KCEGIL

BUREFT

48 Can you change DINE to FEED by altering a single letter at a time?

DINE

_ _ _ _ _ _ _ _ _ _ **Very good**

_ _ _ _ _ _ _ _ _ _ _ _ _ **Retrieve**

_ _ _ _ _ _ _ _ _ _ _ _ **Ward off**

FEED

49 Can you solve the code? There are only seven letters in the message.

SVQAR TBCIN PZXTR

TIEFG IWVCD FYXBK

MTCDO QRAIZ

50 Find the word that links this pair of words.

chain (_____) way

51 Each answer is a four-letter word.
When entered in the grid, a magic square
will be formed in which each word reads
the same across as down.

1 He __ __ __ __ his wallet on the train

2 She plays the __ __ __ __ in an orchestra

3 He is the __ __ __ __ winner in the competition

4 The ants __ __ __ __ in the garden

52 Place every word in the list onto the grid provided.

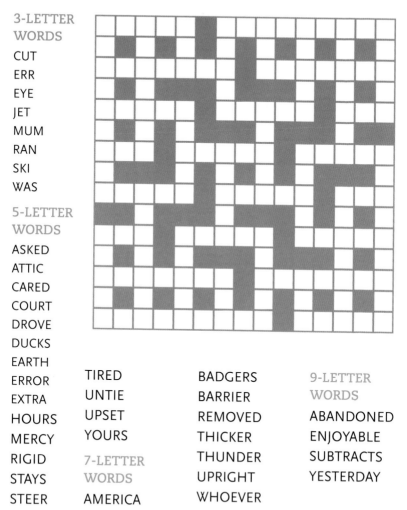

3-LETTER WORDS

CUT
ERR
EYE
JET
MUM
RAN
SKI
WAS

5-LETTER WORDS

ASKED
ATTIC
CARED
COURT
DROVE
DUCKS
EARTH
ERROR
EXTRA
HOURS
MERCY
RIGID
STAYS
STEER
STUNS
TASTY

TIRED
UNTIE
UPSET
YOURS

7-LETTER WORDS

AMERICA

BADGERS
BARRIER
REMOVED
THICKER
THUNDER
UPRIGHT
WHOEVER

9-LETTER WORDS

ABANDONED
ENJOYABLE
SUBTRACTS
YESTERDAY

53 Change TRIM into NEAT by altering a single letter at a time.

TRIM

✎ ----------- **Vehicle**

------------- **Group**

------------- **Nipple**

NEAT

54 Test your vocabulary with this verbal teaser. We've provided four definitions, but only one is correct. Can you find it?

ONYX

Large antelope

Semiprecious stone

Greek god

Inner ear

✎ -------------------------------

55 The dice blocks below each have a six-letter word written on them, but unfortunately you can only see three sides. When you have solved the clues, the first column of the grid will reveal a word.

CLUES

1 Opportunity
2 Clothing
3 Religious reading
4 Deep ravine
5 Father of Saturn
6 Foam
7 Busy
8 Vibration
9 Article
10 Cure

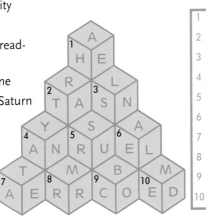

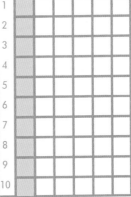

56 Place the tiles in the crossword. The words formed will read the same across as down.

CLUES

1 Arrived
2 Measure of space
3 Cries as a cat
4 Simple

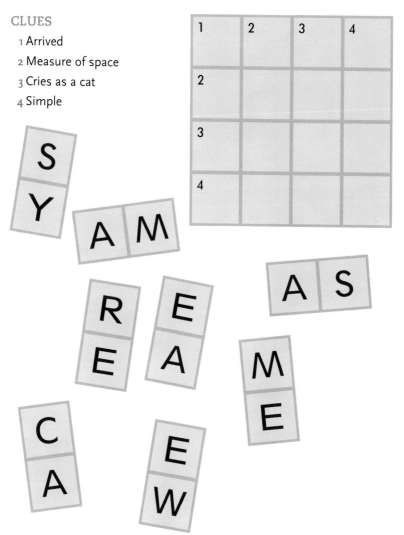

57 Place all the pieces onto the grid so that a valid crossword is formed. Remember that crossword grids possess half-turn symmetry. The colored blocks will also help.

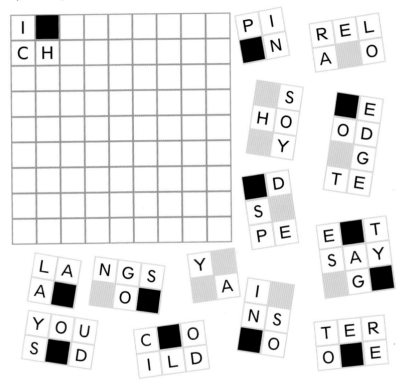

58 Can you find the word in this anagram?

Rain clad

59

Place all the pieces into the grid so that a valid crossword is formed. Remember that crossword grids possess half-turn symmetry. The colored blocks will also help.

60

The wooden blocks each have a six-letter word written on them, but unfortunately you can only see three sides. When you have solved the clues, the first column will reveal a word.

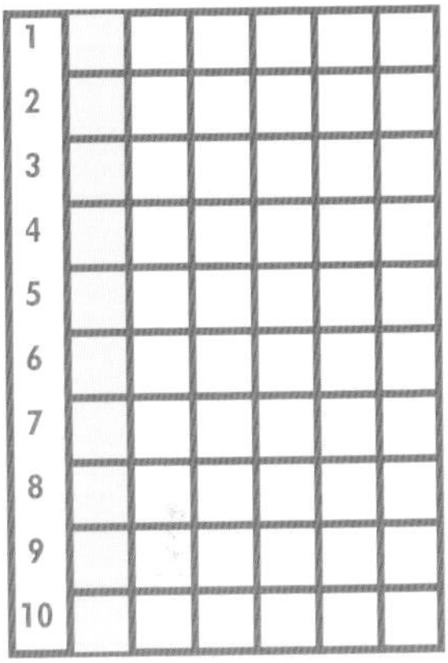

CLUES

1 Conventional
2 Flaming
3 Hallucination
4 Baby
5 Worldwide
6 Symbol of Sagittarius
7 Wood
8 Overlook
9 Choice
10 Relative

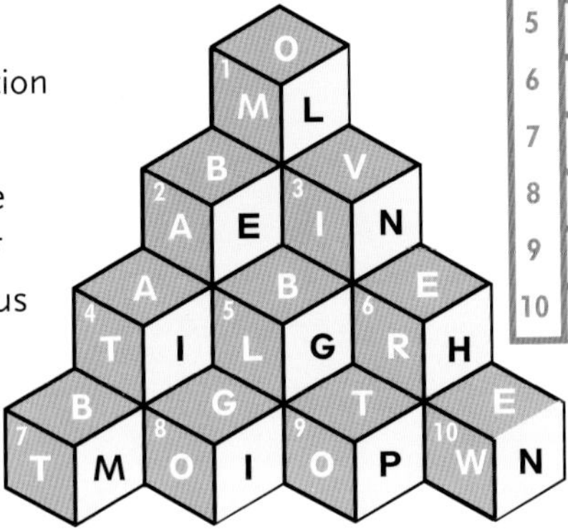

61

There are two ways to solve this magic square, in which the grid reads the same across or down. Answer the clues or fit in the tiles below.

CLUES

1 Identical
2 Afresh
3 Only
4 Sheep

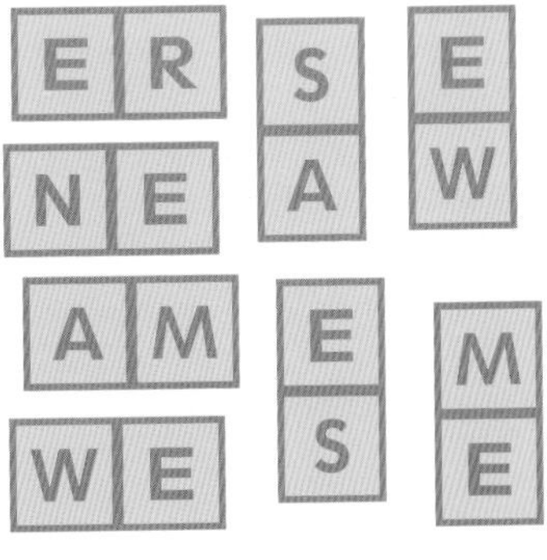

62 In which famous children's story are the following characters found? Think laterally to find the answer.

Colin   Drew

Diana   Len

---

63 Believe it or not, the word LIFELINE is concealed in this grid only once. Can you locate it? It may be read across, down or diagonally in any direction.

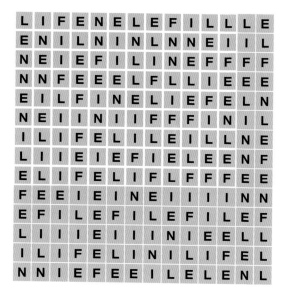

L	I	F	E	N	E	L	E	F	I	L	L	L	E
E	N	I	L	N	I	N	L	N	N	E	I	I	L
N	E	I	E	F	I	L	I	N	E	F	F	F	F
N	N	F	E	E	E	L	F	L	L	I	E	E	E
E	I	L	F	I	N	E	L	I	E	F	E	L	N
N	E	I	I	N	I	I	F	F	F	I	N	I	L
I	L	I	F	E	L	I	L	E	I	L	L	N	E
L	I	I	E	I	E	F	I	E	L	E	E	N	F
E	L	I	F	E	L	I	F	L	F	F	F	E	E
F	E	E	I	E	I	N	E	I	I	I	I	N	N
E	F	I	L	E	F	I	L	E	F	I	L	E	F
L	I	I	I	E	I	I	I	N	I	E	E	L	L
I	L	I	F	E	L	I	N	I	L	I	F	E	L
N	N	I	E	F	E	E	I	L	E	L	E	N	L

64 Which is the odd word out and why?

Bayonet   Pioneer

Colonel   Wronged   Honesty

65 In this alphabetical quiz, we'll take you all 'round the world. Fill in the missing countries from the clues provided.

Clue	Answer
Its flag bears a red maple leaf	_ A _ A _ A
The most easterly Caribbean island	B _ _ B _ _ _ _
N. African country, also a type of leather	_ _ _ _ C C _
"...and Tobago"	_ _ _ _ _ D _ D
In S. America, home of the Angel Falls	_ E _ E _ _ E _ _
Its capital city is Helsinki	F _ _ _ _ _ _
Handed back to China in 1997	_ _ _ G _ _ _ G
If hungry, eat goulash here	H _ _ _ _ _ _
A country with over 1 billion people	I _ _ I _
The river in which Jesus was baptized	J _ _ _ _ _
Important coffee producer	K _ _ _ _ _
Territory subject of a 1982 war	_ _ L _ L _ _ _
	_ _ L _ _ _ _
The current name for Burma	M _ _ _ M _ _
Holland is also called "The..."	N _ _ _ _ _ _ _ N _ _
Formula 1 cars race through its streets	_ O _ _ _ O
Islands, N.E. from Malaysia	P _ _ _ _ P P _ _ _ _
It has large oil deposits	_ _ _ Q
Where Paddington Bear comes from	_ _ R _
It spans 11 time zones	_ _ S S _ _
Eaten at Christmas or Thanksgiving	T _ _ _ _ _
The first World Cup was held here	U _ U _ U _ _
The musical "Miss Saigon" begins here	V _ _ _ _ _ _
Its capital is Cardiff	W _ _ _ _
Where tacos and nachos come from	_ _ X _ _ _
Now lira can't buy you anything here	_ _ _ _ Y
A nut that's hard to crack	_ _ _ Z _ _

66 Insert a word between the brackets that could complete the first word and start the second.

STAGE (_ _ _ _) SOME

67 Can you crack the code to discover what this secret agent has been told to do with the stolen microfilm?

PLAICE YAWN EGGER TIFFIN LOCK AFORE TEA AT

SID KNEE HOPPER A HOW SPITE USE DAY

✎ ---

----

68 Mind your Ps and Qs in this wordsearch for all things grammatical.

ACCENT
ACRONYM
ADJECTIVE
APHORISM
BATHOS
CEDILLA
COLON
COMMA
DATIVE
DIGRAPH
GENDER
GERUNDIVE
MACRON
NEUTER
NOUN
OBJECT

D	I	A	V	D	B	N	O	R	O	M	Y	X	O
P	A	O	P	R	O	T	N	A	C	C	E	N	T
A	L	T	E	H	I	G	L	O	E	G	N	I	V
R	A	V	I	L	O	L	E	V	L	E	L	A	O
X	R	S	D	V	I	R	I	N	L	O	H	C	W
A	U	E	O	D	E	D	I	B	D	P	C	R	E
T	L	M	E	H	N	V	A	S	A	E	E	O	L
N	P	C	O	U	T	L	I	R	M	T	R	N	M
Y	E	D	R	B	L	A	G	T	O	A	E	Y	A
S	R	E	N	Y	J	I	B	U	C	U	G	M	C
A	G	U	S	C	D	E	Q	R	T	E	Y	E	R
X	O	D	A	R	A	P	C	E	R	O	J	D	O
N	A	M	M	O	C	R	R	T	D	A	T	D	N
C	T	E	N	S	E	L	U	G	R	I	V	E	A

OXYMORON QUOTE TENSE VIRGULE

PARADOX SYLLABLE TILDE VOWEL

PLURAL SYNTAX VERB

69 Here's a mixed-up crossword! Can you unravel the anagrams in the clues to find the solutions?

ACROSS

1 Aim into it (9)
6 No bud (5)
7 Debar (5)
9 Deaf (4)
10 Sent in (6)
12 I dream (6)
14 Rats! (4)
17 Ten of (5)
18 Anger (5)
19 Nip thy gal (9)

DOWN

2 No mud (5)
3 Diet (4)
4 Be last (6)
5 Canoe (5)
6 UFO flab (7)
8 Severed (7)
11 Dry ban (6)
13 To Mel (5)
15 No net (5)
16 Char (4)

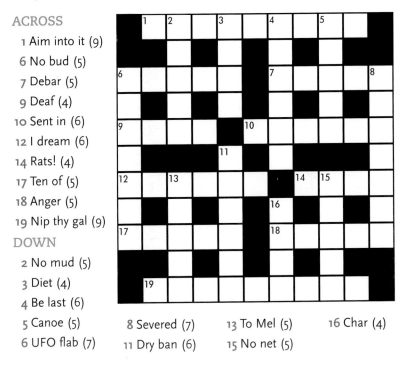

70 What's the answer to this riddle?

What can run, but never walks,

Has a mouth, but never talks.

Has a head, but never weeps,

Has a bed, but never sleeps.

71 Rearrange the letters to make a single word:

SOME GOON

----

72 The answers to the clues are all five-letter words which, when placed correctly into the grid, will form a magic word square in which the same five words can be read both horizontally and vertically. The clues below are in no particular order.

1 Prankster

2 Title of Indian ruler or prince

3 SI unit of frequency

4 On top of

5 Turn aside

73 Unscramble the letters in each circle to produce two words that are synonyms of each other.

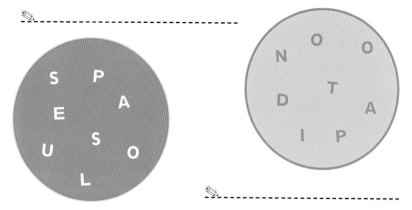

74

Transfer letters between the clues and the grid in order to complete the quotation. The first letter of each answer will also give you the author's name.

			1K	2D		3D	4G	5J
6I	7J	8E	9E		10E	11E	12B	13D	
14J	15G	16B	17A	18D	19H		20F	21B	22H
23H		24H	25C	26J	27K	28E	29A	30H	31G
	32I	33D	34H	35D	36A		37J	38K	
39I	40F	41B	42K	43K	44I	45K		46F	
47H	48C	49A	50K	51K		52G	53A	54K	55C
56G		57K	58I	59G	60J				

A   One-twelfth of a gross — $\overline{36}\ \overline{53}\ \overline{49}\ \overline{17}\ \overline{29}$

B   Listen! — $\overline{21}\ \overline{41}\ \overline{12}\ \overline{16}$

C   Short poem — $\overline{48}\ \overline{55}\ \overline{25}$

D   Bloom — $\overline{2}\ \overline{35}\ \overline{33}\ \overline{3}\ \overline{13}\ \overline{18}$

E   Conduit for surface water — $\overline{9}\ \overline{11}\ \overline{10}\ \overline{28}\ \overline{8}$

F   Levy — $\overline{20}\ \overline{46}\ \overline{40}$

G   You are searching for it! — $\overline{15}\ \overline{59}\ \overline{56}\ \overline{52}\ \overline{31}\ \overline{4}$

H   Debate with others — $\overline{47}\ \overline{22}\ \overline{24}\ \overline{30}\ \overline{34}\ \overline{23}\ \overline{19}$

I   Piece of absorbent cloth — $\overline{6}\ \overline{58}\ \overline{32}\ \overline{39}\ \overline{44}$

J   Gradually declining in power — $\overline{7}\ \overline{37}\ \overline{14}\ \overline{5}\ \overline{26}\ \overline{60}$

K   In a reluctant manner — $\overline{54}\ \overline{38}\ \overline{27}\ \overline{1}\ \overline{42}\ \overline{50}\ \overline{51}\ \overline{43}\ \overline{57}\ \overline{45}$

75 Test your vocabulary with this verbal teaser. We've provided four definitions—but only one is correct. The others are designed to confuse you.

SCARAMOUCH

Volunteer

Boastful coward

Facial disfigurement

Hilltop dwelling

---

76 Test your vocabulary with this verbal teaser. We've provided four definitions for the first word—but only one is correct. The others are designed to confuse you.

PLATYPUS

Greek god

Australian animal

French dish

Indian temple

---

77 One new word could be used to complete the first word and start the second. Can you find it?

MAN (_ _ _ _ _) BARS

78 Can you spot the following herbs in the grid? They may be found across, down or diagonally in any direction and may overlap.

A	N	I	M	A	L	M	A	G	I	C	F	R	Y
C	O	R	I	A	N	D	E	R	H	O	R	S	E
A	G	R	A	R	I	A	N	F	E	N	N	E	L
M	A	E	M	Y	H	T	C	H	A	M	O	I	S
O	R	I	O	N	N	A	I	L	E	A	V	E	R
M	R	I	M	I	N	I	X	Y	L	R	E	Q	A
I	A	R	M	A	D	A	L	L	E	I	X	U	P
L	T	R	O	S	E	V	I	H	C	O	D	O	E
E	E	D	J	O	P	S	C	A	L	A	L	R	Y
E	G	G	R	O	O	B	A	R	R	I	D	E	K
F	A	I	R	R	R	U	G	U	N	S	G	I	
O	V	E	R	H	I	A	C	R	E	A	M	A	W
D	O	E	A	G	L	E	M	I	N	A	H	N	B
A	L	L	I	G	R	Y	R	A	M	E	S	O	R

BASIL	DILL	OREGANO	SORREL
CAMOMILE	FENNEL	PARSLEY	TARRAGON
CHERVIL	LOVAGE	ROSEMARY	THYME
CHIVES	MARJORAM	RUE	
CORIANDER	MINT	SAGE	

79 Travel around this honeycomb crossword and fill up the cells...

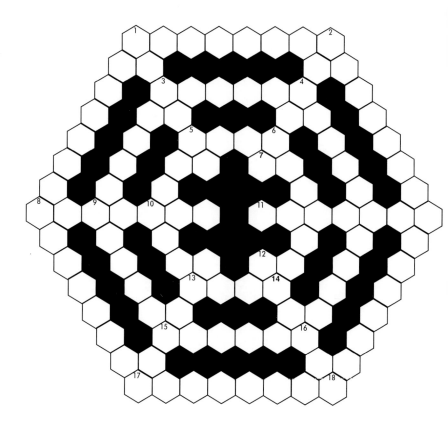

TRAVEL EAST

1 Insect that raises its young in a grid like this (5-3)

3 A perfect place (6)

5 The crest on the head of some male birds (4)

8 A sporting event for rowers (7)

11 The people of Scandinavia 1000 years ago or more (7)

13 A winged insect believed to damage fabrics (4)

15 State in which Las Vegas is located (6)

17 The time by which a task is to be completed (8)

TRAVEL SOUTHEAST

1 The buttock or thigh, a joint of venison (6)

2 A lens to correct the sight (8)

4 The largest river in South America, flowing mostly within Brazil (6)

6 A building used for storing money (4)

8 Transport system in which trains run on iron rails (8)

9 The substance that makes uncooked bread sticky (6)

10 A road vehicle that runs on iron rails (4)

12 A set of words expressing a single idea (6)

TRAVEL NORTHEAST

7 On fire, bright and shiny (6)

8 Study to try to discover something new about a subject (8)

9 A large rich cake, often filled with cream (6)

10 French chalk, a soft powder used in cosmetics (4)

14 A small bird of prey with very good eyesight (4)

16 Reddish-brown hair (6)

17 A machine for generating electricity (6)

18 Very, very large (8)

80 Which word means the opposite of elevate?

Dissolve

Lower

Ventilate

Levitate

✎ -

81 Test your vocabulary with this verbal teaser. We've provided four definitions— but only one is correct. The others are designed to confuse you.

VOLATILE

Mighty   Sleepy

Flighty   Creepy

✎ -

82 The dice blocks each have a six-letter word written on them, but, unfortunately, you can see only three sides. When you have solved the clues, the first column will reveal a 10-letter word.

CLUES

1 Place of worship
2 Acquire
3 Learner
4 Conclude
5 Stimulate
6 Bring down
7 Go by
8 Sprightly
9 Luck
10 Armed guard

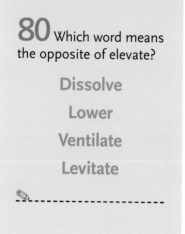

Memory & Visual Puzzles

83 Which of the boxed symbols completes the set?

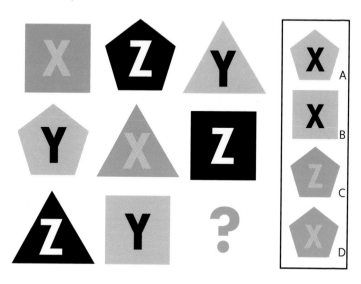

84 What percentage of this grid is orange and what percentage is white?

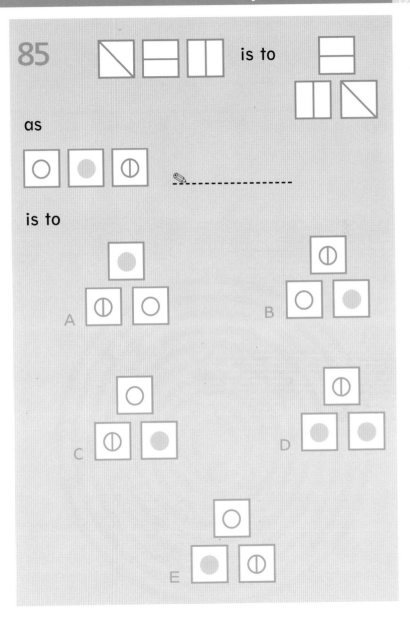

86 Which arrow comes next in the sequence?

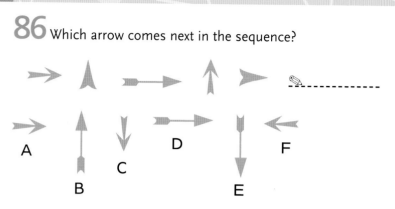

87 Can you find your way to the middle of this circular maze without going google-eyed?

88 Place nine coins on this board as shown. Take any coin and make it jump (via any horizontal, vertical or diagonal move) to land on an empty square on the other side. When a coin is jumped, remove it from the board. The aim is to remove eight coins from the board, similar to a game of solitaire. Extra kudos if you can get the final piece to land back in the central square!

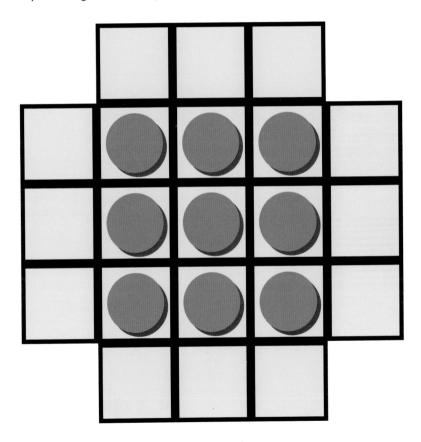

89 Can you divide the picture on the right by drawing three straight lines to produce five sections, each containing one spiral shell, two stars and three squares?

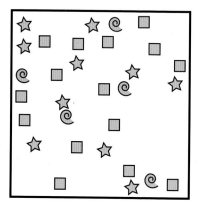

90 When the shape on the right is folded to form a cube, which is the only one of the following that cannot be produced?

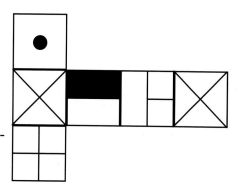

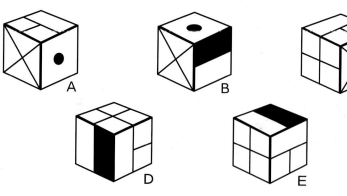

A   B   C

D   E

91 Three dice are arranged side by side. Seven faces are visible. What is the total of the other 11 sides?

✎ --

92 Expressed as a fraction, what area of this hexagon is shaded?

✎ --

93 Can you spot the seven differences between these two pictures? Circle them in the drawing on the right.

94 Which of the four boxed symbols completes the set?

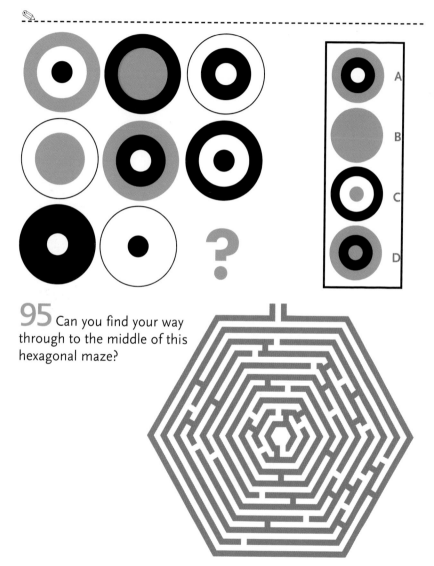

95 Can you find your way through to the middle of this hexagonal maze?

96 Below are six shapes, each with a different number in the center. Study the shapes for 1 minute then see if you can answer the questions below.

Can you answer these questions to the puzzle on this page without looking back?

✎ _ _ _ _ _ _ _ _ _ _ _ _ _ _ _ _ _ 1 Which shape is first in the sequence?

_ _ _ _ _ _ _ _ _ _ _ _ _ _ _ _ _ _ 2 Which shape has a number 1 in it?

_ _ _ _ _ _ _ _ _ _ _ _ _ _ _ _ _ _ 3 What number is inside the square?

_ _ _ _ _ _ _ _ _ _ _ _ _ _ _ _ _ _ 4 How many sides does the top right shape have?

_ _ _ _ _ _ _ _ _ _ _ _ _ _ _ _ _ _ 5 What number is inside the triangle?

_ _ _ _ _ _ _ _ _ _ _ _ _ _ _ _ _ _ 6 How many sides do the last two shapes have between them?

7 What shape comes first on the second row?

_ _ _ _ _ _ _ _ _ _ _ _ _ _ _ _ _
_ _ _ _ _ _ _ _ _ _ _ _ _ _ _ _ _ 8 What do you get if you subtract the number in the first shape from the sum of the numbers in the other shapes?

97 Can you divide this picture by drawing two straight lines to produce three sections, each containing three nuts and five screws?

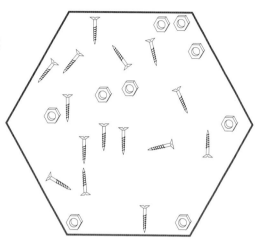

98 Solve the sequence to see if you're visually minded.

What comes next?

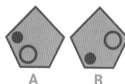

A   B   C

D

99 Using three different colors (or labeling the areas using three different symbols), shade in the diagram so no two areas that share a border are the same color.

100 How many revolutions must the large cog make to return all the cogs to their starting position?

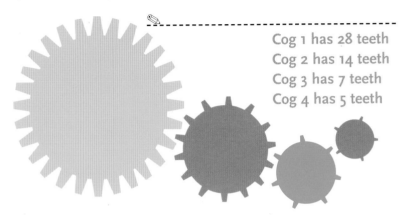

Cog 1 has 28 teeth
Cog 2 has 14 teeth
Cog 3 has 7 teeth
Cog 4 has 5 teeth

101 In the following group of dominoes, which one is missing?

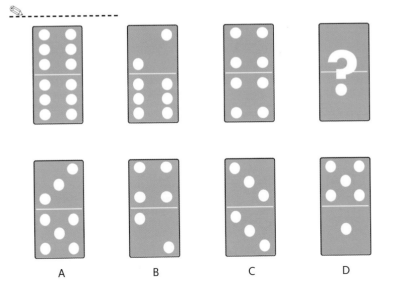

A   B   C   D

102 Using three different colors (or labeling the areas using three different symbols), shade in this picture so no two areas that share a border are the same color.

103 When the shape on the right is folded to form a cube, which is the only one of the following that cannot be produced?

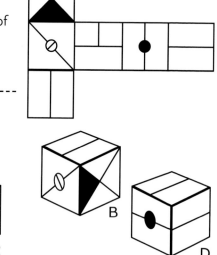

104 There is something wrong with one of these dice. Can you spot which one?

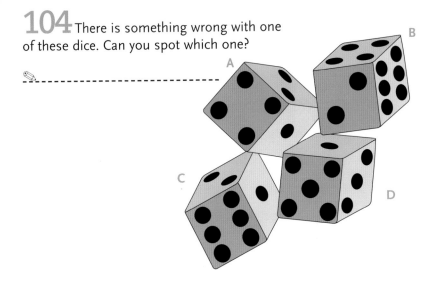

105 How many squares are there altogether in this diagram? There may be many more than you at first think.

106 Which of the four boxed figures completes the set?

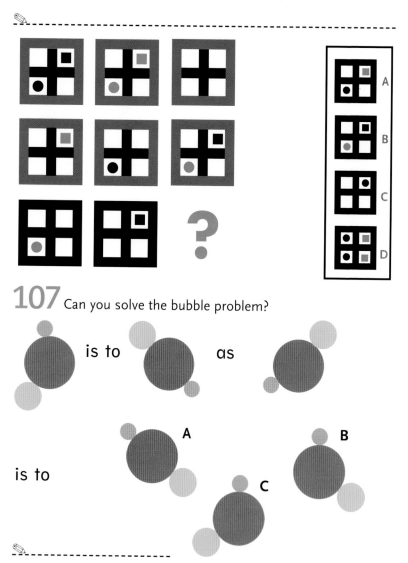

107 Can you solve the bubble problem?

is to ... as ...

is to ...

108 Can you find the odd
one out and why?

✎ -----------------------

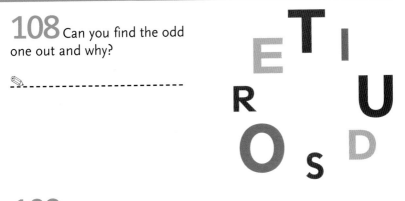

109 Can you find your way through to the middle of this
square maze?

110

There are ten dominoes in this wall, but five have been masked out. Can you place the missing dominoes correctly, bearing in mind that each vertical line of four numbers (as well as the two end vertical lines of two numbers) adds up to eight?

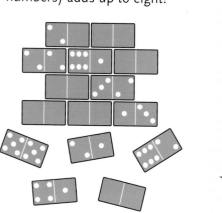

111

Which are the only two pieces that will fit together perfectly to form a complete triangle?

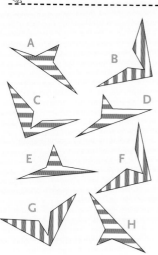

112

Can you discover which windmill is the odd one out and why?

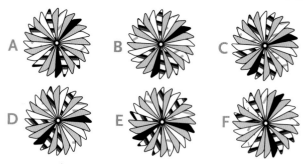

113 Can you crack the code and discover where you might find a Swiss spy?

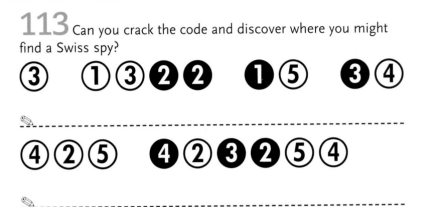

114 What is the value of the missing domino?

115 At first glance, these spinning tops may look the same, but only two are identical. Which is the matching pair?

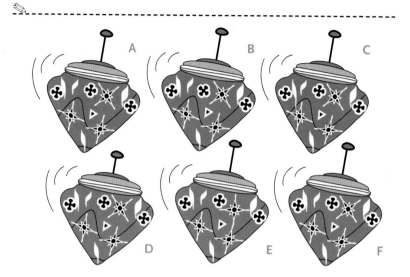

116 How many squares are there in this diagram?

117 When the shape at the right is folded to form a cube, which if any of the following can be produced?

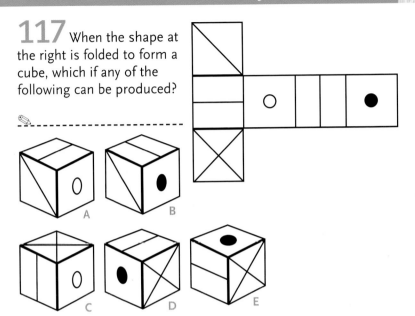

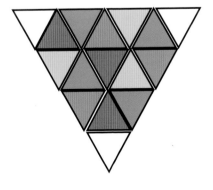

118 What colors should be in the corners?

119 What is the sum total of the dots on the eleven hidden sides of these three dice?

120 Can you divide this picture by drawing three straight lines to produce four sections, each containing eight different traffic signs?

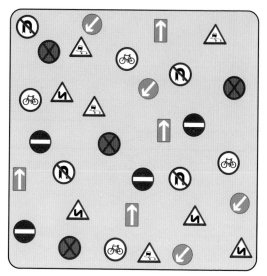

121 Which of the boxed symbols completes the set?

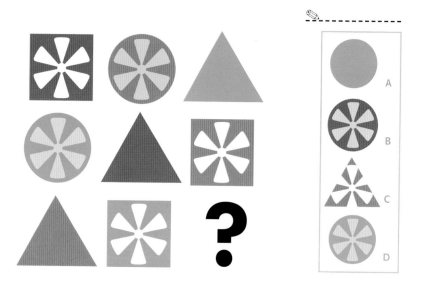

122 When the shape below is folded to form a cube, just one of the following can be produced. Which one?

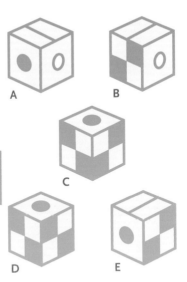

A

B

C

D

E

123 Can you divide this picture by drawing two straight lines to produce four sections, each containing four bees facing in different directions?

124 Which of the four boxed figures completes the set?

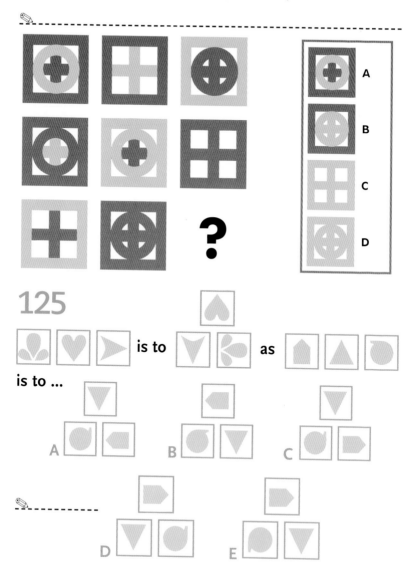

125

is to ... as ... is to ...

A B C

D E

126 Can you help the young penguins reach their mother in the cave before the polar bear gets too close? Start at the pointer and don't forget to wear something warm!

127 When this shape is folded to form a cube, just one of the following can be produced. Which one?

A

B

C

D

E

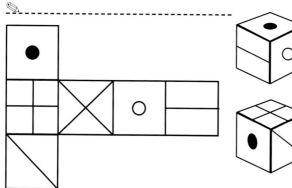

128 Can you divide the picture on the right by drawing five straight lines to produce eleven sections, each containing two different shapes?

129

The six items below may look similar, but only two are identical. Can you spot which two?

130

When the shape below is folded to form a cube, just one of the following can be produced. Which one?

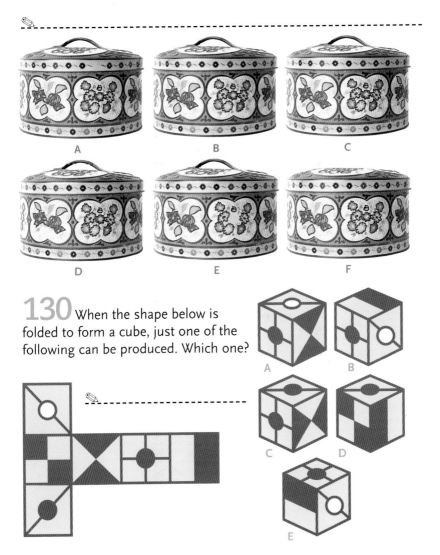

A

B

C

D

E

131 Which of the four boxed figures completes the set?

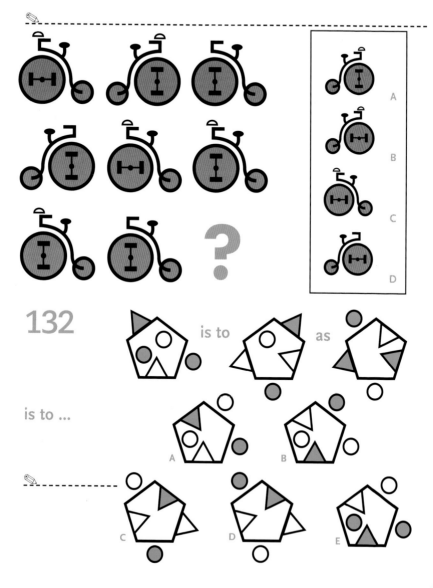

132

is to ... as ...

is to ...

133 Which domino (A, B, C or D) should fill the empty space?

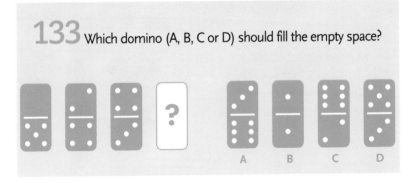

134 In the puzzle below, which lettered clock (A, B, C or D) replaces the question mark?

135 Can you divide this picture by drawing two straight lines to produce three sections, each containing two apples, two lemons, two pears, a banana and an orange?

136 There are eight very subtle differences between these two pictures. Can you spot them? Circle them in the lower drawing.

137 Move four coins to make a new, smaller square with three coins in each row and column.

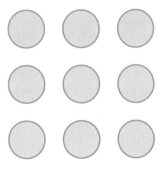

138 Using four colors (or symbols), color (or label) each circle so that no two connected circles contain the same color/symbol. Each color or symbol must be used for exactly four circles.

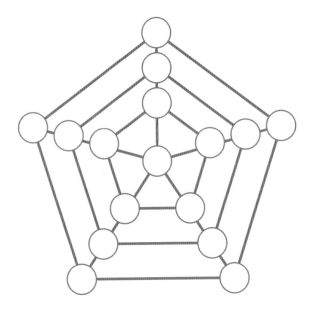

139 Ten dominoes have been used to build this wall, but six have been masked out. Can you place the missing dominoes correctly, bearing in mind that each vertical line of four numbers (as well as the two end vertical lines of two numbers) adds up to nine?

140 In the puzzle below, which of the lettered alternatives (A, B, C or D) fits into the empty space?

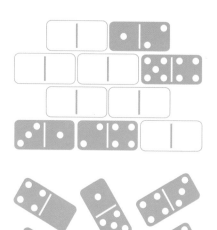

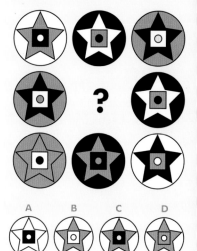

141 Which are the only two pieces that will fit together to form a perfect copy of this green shape? Pieces may be rotated, but they may not be flipped over.

A

B

C

D

E

142 When the shape below is folded to form a cube, just two of the following can be produced. Which two?

A

B

C

D

E

143 Should the middle circle be blue or white?

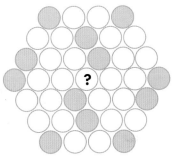

?

144 Here's Freddie Fisher, sitting on the bank of the Catchmore River, dreaming of the fish he'll hook. Can you divide his thoughts opposite by drawing two straight lines to produce three sections, each containing four small fish, three medium fish and two large fish?

145 Each umbrella is one of a matching pair: an umbrella and its reflection, as it would appear if held up to a mirror. However, one has no companion umbrella. Which is the odd one out?

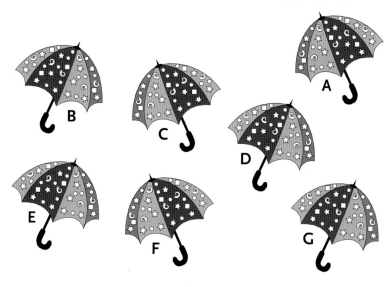

146 The trick here is to get from the top of this maze to the bottom.

147 A standard set of 28 dominoes has been laid out as shown. One is already in position, to give you a start. Can you draw in the edges of the rest? The check-box on the right has been provided as an aid. Remember that dominoes can be placed two ways.

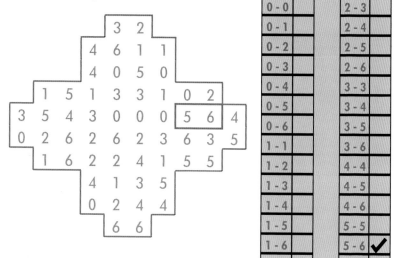

0 - 0			2 - 3	
0 - 1			2 - 4	
0 - 2			2 - 5	
0 - 3			2 - 6	
0 - 4			3 - 3	
0 - 5			3 - 4	
0 - 6			3 - 5	
1 - 1			3 - 6	
1 - 2			4 - 4	
1 - 3			4 - 5	
1 - 4			4 - 6	
1 - 5			5 - 5	
1 - 6			5 - 6	✔
2 - 2			6 - 6	

148 Can you divide the picture by drawing four straight lines to produce seven sections, each containing a square, a circle and a star?

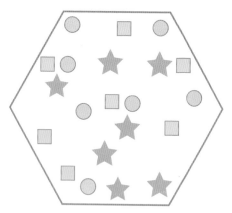

149 There's a fishy tale below—but the pictures are in the wrong order. Can you put them into the right order to discover what surprise was waiting for this fisherman?

1

2

3

4

5

6

7

8

9

150 When the shape below is folded to form a cube, just two of the following can be produced. Which two?

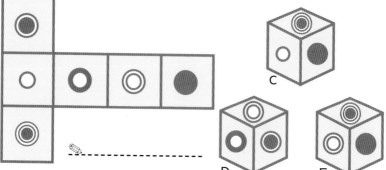

A B C D E

151 You must always move two touching coins without separating them. What is the least number of moves you can make to leave all six coins below touching with alternate heads and tails?

Number Puzzles

152 Each block is equal to the sum of the two numbers beneath it. Find all the missing numbers.

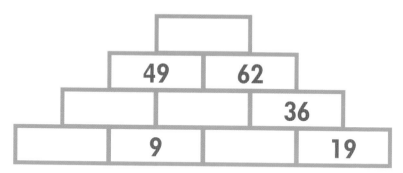

153 To complete this numbersearch you first need to find the answers to the questions below. Next, locate the numbers in the grid. They may be read up, down, backward, forward or diagonally.

1 1500 + 727

2 1,000,000 ÷ 50

3 2132 ÷ 2

4 500 x 500

5 9876 - 4444

6 28,2828 - 10,101

7 69,999 + 3

8 20,202 ÷ 2

9 9669 ÷ 3

10 101 x 55

11 858 - 101

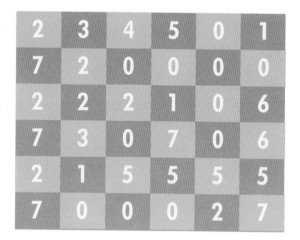

154 Make your way from the top red hexagon to the bottom one, creating a working sum that totals 10. You must alternate between numbers and symbols and may not visit the same hexagon twice.

155 Which is the odd number out, and why?

2378, 4589, 1368, 3798, 4789

✎ --

156 These two rockets are on a collision course in the same orbit around the sun. Rocket A is taking 15 months to orbit the sun, while Rocket B makes an orbit every 12 months. How long do the scientists have to reprogram the rockets before they crash?

✎ --

157 At the start of the Kentucky Derby, I correctly counted the numbers of horses' legs plus the number of riders' legs and the total came to 168. How many horses were there in the race altogether?

----

158 Place a number in the middle box by which all the other numbers can be divided without leaving a remainder. The number is greater than 1.

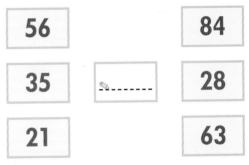

56		84
35		28
21		63

159 Which three of the four pieces below can be fitted together to form a perfect square?

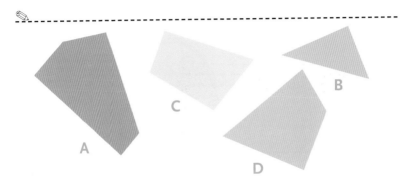

160 The number 13579 appears just once in this wordsearch-style grid and occurs in a straight line, running either backward or forward in either a horizontal, vertical or diagonal direction. Can you locate it?

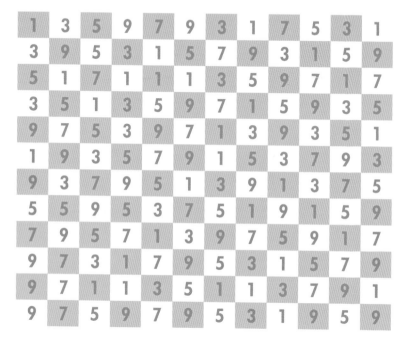

1	3	5	9	7	9	3	1	7	5	3	1
3	9	5	3	1	5	7	9	3	1	5	9
5	1	7	1	1	1	3	5	9	7	1	7
3	5	1	3	5	9	7	1	5	9	3	5
9	7	5	3	9	7	1	3	9	3	5	1
1	9	3	5	7	9	1	5	3	7	9	3
9	3	7	9	5	1	3	9	1	3	7	5
5	5	9	5	3	7	5	1	9	1	5	9
7	9	5	7	1	3	9	7	5	9	1	7
9	7	3	1	7	9	5	3	1	5	7	9
9	7	1	1	3	5	1	1	3	7	9	1
9	7	5	9	7	9	5	3	1	9	5	9

161 Complete the sum below using one each of all the numbers and signs in the circle.

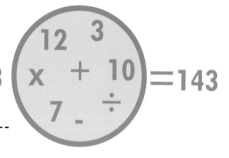

33 (12 3 x + 10 7 ÷ -) = 143

162 Place a number in the central box by which all the other numbers can be divided without leaving a remainder. The number is greater than 1.

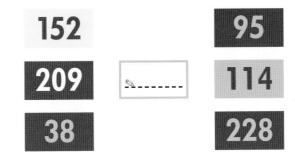

163 Replace the question marks with three different mathematical symbols (+, -, ÷ or x) to get the right answer.

28 ? 7 ? 3 ? 5 = 17

✎ --

164 How many stars are needed to balance scale C?

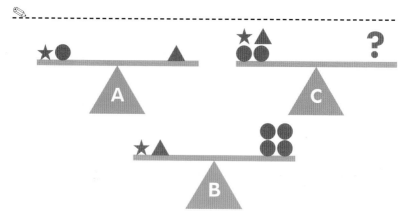

And in this teaser, how many circles are needed to balance C?

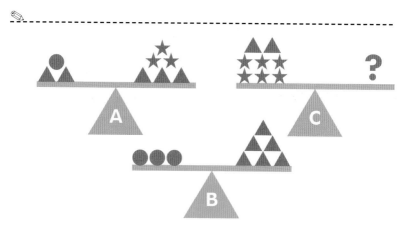

165 How many minutes is it before 12 noon if 40 minutes ago it was three times as many minutes past 9 a.m.?

166 Can you fit these numbers into the grid? One number has been inserted to help you get started.

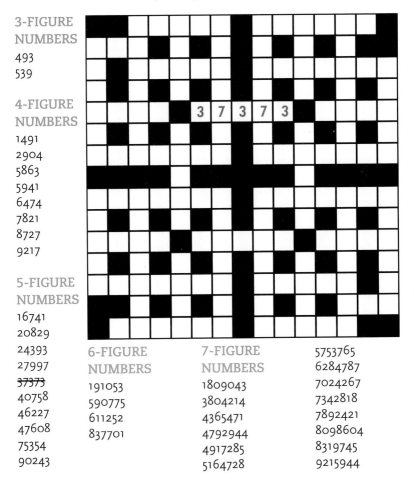

3-FIGURE NUMBERS
493
539

4-FIGURE NUMBERS
1491
2904
5863
5941
6474
7821
8727
9217

5-FIGURE NUMBERS
16741
20829
24393
27997
37373
40758
46227
47608
75354
90243

6-FIGURE NUMBERS
191053
590775
611252
837701

7-FIGURE NUMBERS
1809043
3804214
4365471
4792944
4917285
5164728
5753765
6284787
7024267
7342818
7892421
8098604
8319745
9215944

167 A magic square has the special property that the sum of all the numbers in each row, column and both main diagonals equals the same number. With this in mind, complete this magic square so that it contains nine consecutive numbers.

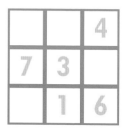

168 The hour hand on the fourth clock is missing. Follow the sequence to discover the number to which it should point.

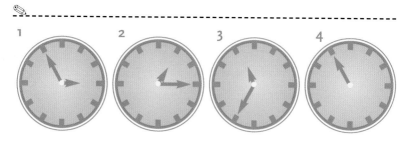

169 Which is the odd number out and why?

481, 296, 384, 479, 387, 794, 926, 148, 843

170 Each block in this pyramid is the total of the two blocks below it. Can you find all the missing numbers?

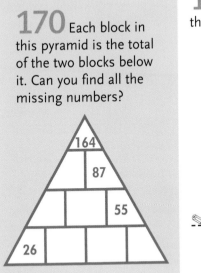

171 Think laterally to find the missing number.

PORTUGAL = 51
EGYPT = 31
CANADA = 39
ETHIOPIA = 53
AMERICA = 46
ENGLAND = ?

172 What is the total value of the angles in an octagon?

173 Replace the question marks with mathematical symbols to produce the correct answer. Only two of the four mathematical signs, +, -, ÷ and x, are used.

$$35 \; ? \; 7 \; ? \; 14 \; ? \; 4 = 7$$

174 Rockets A and B are orbiting different suns. Rocket A takes six months to perform one orbit, while Rocket B takes 28 months. At the moment, the middle of both rockets is precisely aligned on the line between the suns. How long will it be before this situation arises once again?

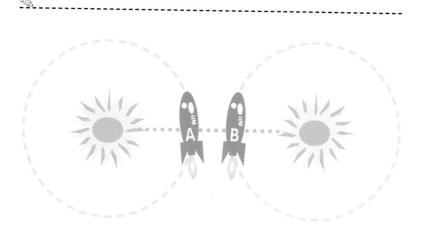

175 Complete the sum below using every one of the numbers and signs in the circle.

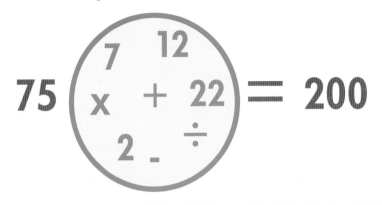

$$75 \left(\begin{array}{c} 7 \quad 12 \\ x \quad + \quad 22 \\ 2 \quad \div \\ . \end{array} \right) = 200$$

176 Each row and column contains the same numbers and symbols, but they are arranged in a different order each time. Can you find the correct order to arrive at the final totals shown?

7	+	1	x	3	–	4	=	20
							=	18
							=	12
							=	6
=		=		=		=		
8		24		15		26		

177 Which number comes next?

10, 1, 8, 3, 6, 5, ?

----

178 The totals of the following equations can all be found in our wordsearch-style grid reading up, down, backward, forward or diagonally. The bravest won't resort to a calculator!

1 33 × 33
2 999 + 999
3 5 × 5 × 5 × 5 × 5
4 382 ÷ 2
5 (1000 ÷ 50) × 99
6 321 × 123
7 77 × 77
8 22222 × 4
9 199 × 5
10 (8 × 8) + (7 × 7)
11 (44 + 44) × (33 + 33)
12 3240 ÷ 18
13 143 × 7

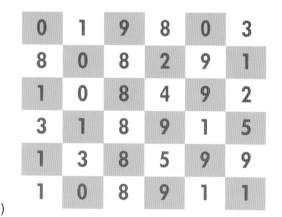

179 The answers to the general knowledge questions below can be found somewhere—in the correct sequence—in the column of digits on the right. The answers are 2, 3 or 4 digits in length.

1	Degrees in three right angles	18052700
2	Years of marriage for a diamond anniversary	40505560
3	Isotope of uranium used in an atomic bomb	12356789
4	Minutes in a day	36214402
5	Cost of the utility spaces in Monopoly	12001500
6	Number of the White House on Pennsylvania Avenue	61600919
7	Age to which Methuselah lived	74519690
8	Number for a hurricane on the Beaufort Scale	12351022
9	Minutes of sound held on a standard CD	41037457
10	Number of human chromosomes	23482460

180 In the domino sequence below, which of the options (A, B, C or D) should replace the question mark?

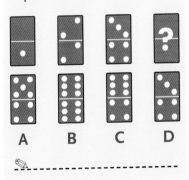

A   B   C   D

181 Imagine giant dominoes in place of standing stones in the celebrated sacred circle of Stonehenge.

If the numerical value of each horizontal domino is equal to the total value of the two dominoes supporting it, can you arrange the nine dominoes (below) in the correct configuration?

182 Place the tiles into the grid so that

(a) the tiles in the first row are the same as the first column, the tiles in the second row are the same as the second column, and so on

(b) each row and column contains two squares of each color

(c) each row and column contains two of each number.

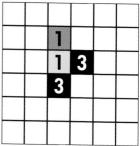

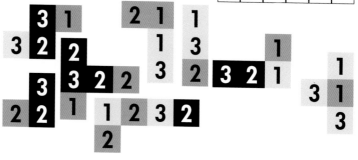

183 Which number should replace the question mark in the bottom box?

184 Each block in this pyramid is the total of the two blocks below it. Can you find all the missing numbers?

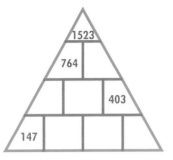

185 The minute hand on the fourth clock is missing. To which number should it be pointing?

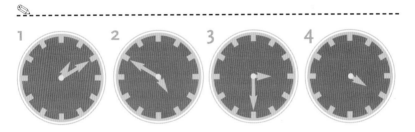

186 Which number is the odd one out and why?

34102, 76304, 46138, 85255, 59177

187 Place the six numbers in the list on the triangle to make each of the three sides add up to the same total.

4 5 6 7 8 9

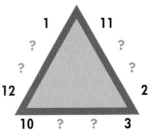

188

Can you fit these numbers into the grid? One number has already been positioned to help you.

3-FIGURE NUMBERS
~~698~~
744

4-FIGURE NUMBERS
1217
2046
2268
2586
3168
3735
4584
8603

5-FIGURE NUMBERS
10131
18887
21858
59421
61525
72263
84207
84471
84747
89455

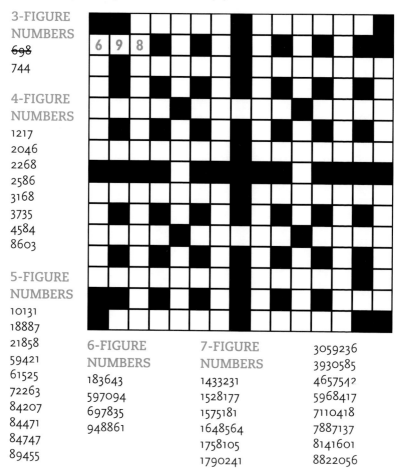

6-FIGURE NUMBERS
183643
597094
697835
948861

7-FIGURE NUMBERS
1433231
1528177
1575181
1648564
1758105
1790241

3059236
3930585
4657542
5968417
7110418
7887137
8141601
8822056

189 The totals of the following equations can all be found in our wordsearch-style grid reading up, down, backward, forward or diagonally. The bravest won't resort to a calculator!

1 1111 x 9

2 20 x 20 x 20

3 88 x 88

4 22 x 222

5 1776 ÷ 4

6 3 x 3030

7 1010 ÷ 5

8 (3 x 3 x 3) x (4 x 4 x 4)

9 (5 x 5) x (5 x 5 x 5)

10 7 x 200

11 4994 x 2

12 66000 ÷ 3

13 23624 x 5

5	2	1	3	2	0
4	4	7	7	0	2
8	8	9	9	2	1
8	0	9	0	4	8
4	9	0	0	4	1
9	0	9	0	4	1

190 Replace the question marks with mathematical symbols to produce the correct answer. Only the mathematical signs +, -, ÷ and x may be used. Can you find two possible solutions?

8 ? 3 ? 2 ? 5 = 17

191 Each block in this pyramid is the total of the two blocks below it. Which number should replace the question mark in the bottom row?

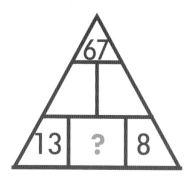

192 If the yellow and white areas of this flag are of equal areas, how wide is the yellow stripe at point x?

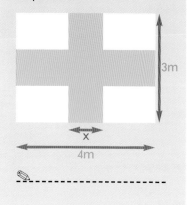

193 The minute hand on the fourth clock is missing. To which number should it be pointing?

194 The number 8283531 appears just once in this wordsearch-style grid and occurs in a straight line, running either backward or forward in either a horizontal, vertical or diagonal direction. Can you locate it?

8	1	1	3	5	3	2	8	8	1	3	1
8	2	3	5	3	1	8	2	2	8	5	3
2	8	5	2	8	5	2	8	3	8	2	5
8	3	2	3	8	2	8	3	2	2	2	3
3	5	8	8	5	2	3	8	8	1	8	5
5	3	3	2	3	5	3	1	5	5	2	2
1	1	5	8	8	5	1	8	8	3	5	8
1	3	3	5	3	8	2	2	8	5	3	8
2	5	1	1	2	8	3	1	5	3	1	3
8	2	8	3	5	2	1	2	3	1	2	5
8	3	2	8	1	2	5	3	8	2	8	3
1	8	1	3	8	3	5	2	8	8	5	1

195 Make a sum totaling 359 using the numbers in the circle and any of the four standard mathematical operations (+, -, x, ÷).

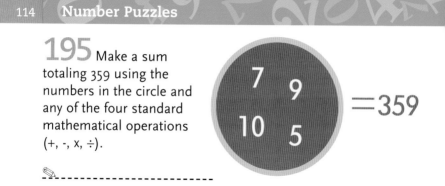

=359

✎ --------------------------------

196 Which numbers should replace the question marks?

✎ --

197

Give yourself 15 minutes for these mental arithmetic challenges and see how you do!

1 Which is greater, millimeters in a mile or seconds in November?

    ✎---

2 If 1 gallon = 4.5 liters, how many milliliters are there in 5 gallons?

    ✎---

3 What is 10% of 20% of 30% of 40% of 5,000?

    ✎---

4 What is a score plus a gross plus a baker's dozen?

    ✎---

5 In the sum below, the same number appears in both boxes. If it is not 2, what is it?

$$\square \times \square = 4$$

    ✎---

6 Paul is 40 and his daughter Jane is 13. How many years ago was Paul four times as old as Jane?

    ✎---

7 Which three numbers total the same when they are added as when they are multiplied together?

    ✎---

8 If 2 rabbits eat 4 carrots, how many carrots do 1 1/2 rabbits eat?

    ✎---

198 Can you fit these numbers into the grid? One number has already been positioned to help you.

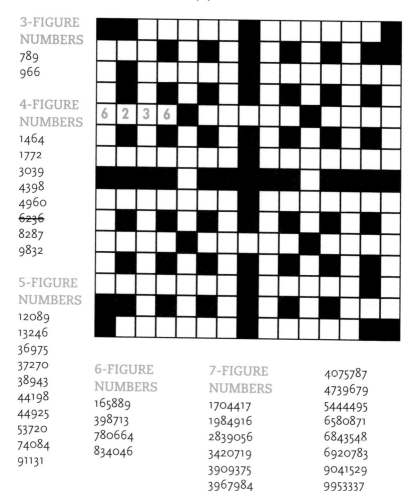

3-FIGURE NUMBERS
789
966

4-FIGURE NUMBERS
1464
1772
3039
4398
4960
6236
8287
9832

5-FIGURE NUMBERS
12089
13246
36975
37270
38943
44198
44925
53720
74084
91131

6-FIGURE NUMBERS
165889
398713
780664
834046

7-FIGURE NUMBERS
1704417
1984916
2839056
3420719
3909375
3967984

4075787
4739679
5444495
6580871
6843548
6920783
9041529
9953337

199 A magic square has the special property that all the numbers in each row, column and both main diagonals add up to the same number. With this in mind, complete this magic square.

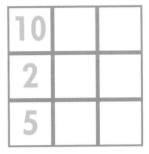

200 If a quarter of a square is taken from a corner, can you dissect the remaining area into four parts, each of the same shape and size?

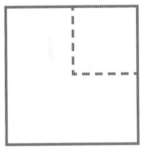

201 What comes next in this number sequence?

6, 17, 50, 149, 446, ?

202 Place a number in the middle box by which all the other numbers can be divided without leaving a remainder. The answer is greater than 1.

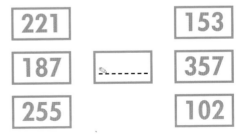

221   153

187   357

255   102

203 Rockets A and B are orbiting different suns. Rocket A takes 6 months to complete one orbit, while rocket B takes 15 months. How long will it be before the middle of both rockets is precisely aligned on the line that joins both suns?

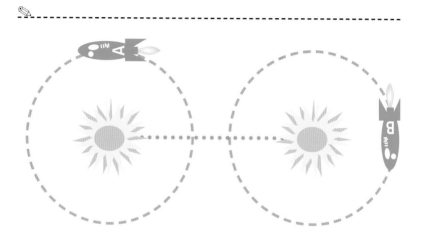

204 Which number should replace the question mark?

81, 82, 80, 240, 60, 61, 59, ?

205 What is the missing number?

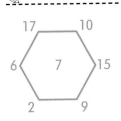
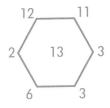
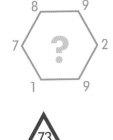

206

Each block in this pyramid is the total of the two blocks below it. Can you find all the missing numbers (fractions are included)?

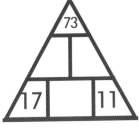

207

Each block in this pyramid is the total of the two blocks below it. Can you find all the missing numbers?

208

Can you cut this trapezoid into four smaller trapezoids of the same shape?

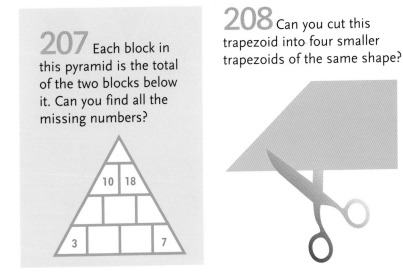

209 Place a number (greater than 1) in the middle box by which all the other numbers can be divided without leaving a remainder.

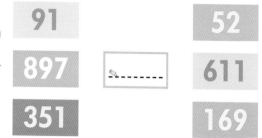

210 What percentage of this triangle is green and what percentage is white?

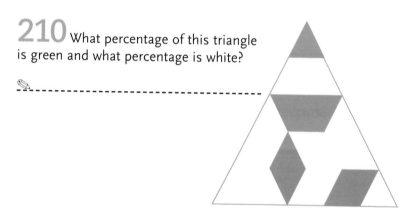

211 Place a number in the middle box by which all the other numbers can be divided without leaving a remainder. The answer is greater than 1.

212 There were 16 runners in the cross-country race numbered 1 to 16 but I did not see the winner, so I asked six spectators for the number of the winner. These were their answers:

A   The number was odd.

B   The number was even.

C   The number was prime.

D   The number was square.

E   The number was made up of straight lines.

F   The number was composed of double digits.

But only four had told the truth.

What was the most likely number of the winner? ✎ _ _ _ _ _ _ _ _ _ _ _ _

Note: 1 is not considered to be a prime number.

213 Each row and column contains the same numbers and symbols, but they are arranged in a different order each time. Find the correct order to arrive at the final totals shown.

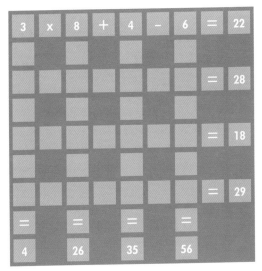

214 How many forks are needed to balance scale C?

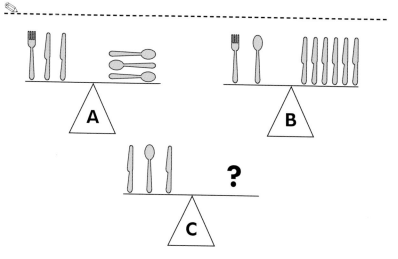

215 Can you divide the box below by drawing four straight lines to produce five sections, so that the numbers in each part add up to 12?

```
3   8        8    1

      1    2      3

        6      9
          1      7
2
      4      3   2
```

216 Which is the odd number out and why?

6472

3297

9782

3964

8342

217 Each block is equal to the sum of the two numbers beneath it. Find all the missing numbers.

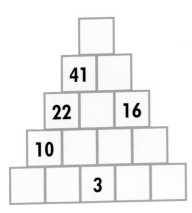

218 How good are you at solving mathematical problems?

A father agreed to pay his son for his math homework: 8 cents for every correct answer, a fine of 5 cents for every incorrect solution. At the end of 26 problems, neither owes anything to the other.

How many problems did the boy solve correctly?

219 Make a calculation whose total is the figure on the right using some or all of the numbers in the circle with any of the four standard mathematical operations (+, -, x and ÷).

3
6   25
8
10   75

=321

220 Which clock is the odd one out and why?

A   B   C   D

221 How many revolutions must the large cog make to return all the cogs to their starting positions?

Cog 1 has 17 teeth

Cog 2 has 12 teeth

Cog 3 has 5 teeth

Cog 4 has 4 teeth

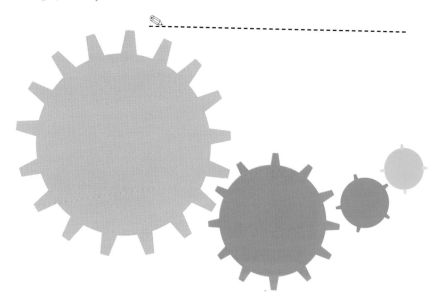

222 The number 2163767 appears just once in this number-search grid and occurs in a straight line, running either backward or forward in a horizontal, vertical or diagonal direction. Can you locate it?

2	7	6	7	2	1	6	3	6	7	6	7
7	1	2	6	3	1	2	7	7	6	3	1
7	6	6	6	1	7	3	2	3	1	7	6
3	7	3	7	6	7	1	6	2	6	7	2
6	3	6	1	6	3	7	2	7	6	1	1
7	7	2	3	6	7	6	7	3	6	1	2
1	3	1	7	7	2	1	3	7	3	6	7
2	2	7	1	2	1	2	7	6	1	2	3
3	6	1	7	7	3	1	3	7	1	7	6
2	1	3	6	7	6	3	7	6	3	2	1
7	6	7	6	3	7	1	2	3	7	1	3
2	1	3	6	7	6	3	7	1	3	6	2

223 Can you divide the picture below by drawing two straight lines to produce three sections, so that the numbers in one part add up to 12, those in another part add up to 13 and those in a third part add up to 14? No part may contain identical digits.

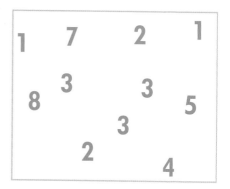

224 What is the value of the missing domino?

225 Can you fit these numbers into the grid? One number has already been given to help you.

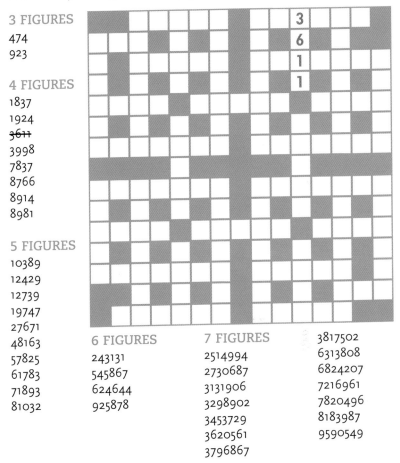

3 FIGURES
474
923

4 FIGURES
1837
1924
3611
3998
7837
8766
8914
8981

5 FIGURES
10389
12429
12739
19747
27671
48163
57825
61783
71893
81032

6 FIGURES
243131
545867
624644
925878

7 FIGURES
2514994
2730687
3131906
3298902
3453729
3620561
3796867
3817502
6313808
6824207
7216961
7820496
8183987
9590549

226 Every row and column contains the same numbers and symbols, but they are arranged in a different order each time. Find the correct order to arrive at the final totals shown.

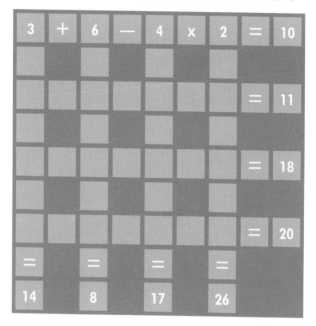

3	+	6	—	4	x	2	=	10
							=	11
							=	18
							=	20
=		=		=		=		
14		8		17		26		

227 Each block is equal to the sum of the two numbers beneath it. Find all the missing numbers.

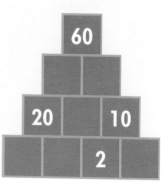

228 The number 1956345 appears just once in this number-search grid and occurs in a straight line, running either backward or forward in a horizontal, vertical or diagonal direction. Can you locate it?

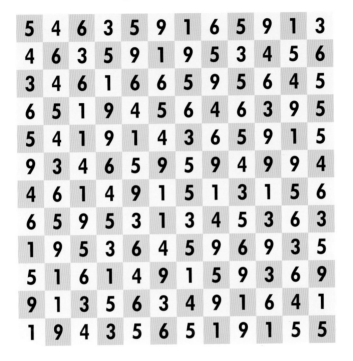

5	4	6	3	5	9	1	6	5	9	1	3
4	6	3	5	9	1	9	5	3	4	5	6
3	4	6	1	6	6	5	9	5	6	4	5
6	5	1	9	4	5	6	4	6	3	9	5
5	4	1	9	1	4	3	6	5	9	1	5
9	3	4	6	5	9	5	9	4	9	9	4
4	6	1	4	9	1	5	1	3	1	5	6
6	5	9	5	3	1	3	4	5	3	6	3
1	9	5	3	6	4	5	9	6	9	3	5
5	1	6	1	4	9	1	5	9	3	6	9
9	1	3	5	6	3	4	9	1	6	4	1
1	9	4	3	5	6	5	1	9	1	5	5

229 Replace the question marks with mathematical symbols to produce the correct answer. Only the four standard operations (+, -, x and ÷) are permitted. Perform calculations in strict left to right order. Can you find two possible ways of reaching the solution?

$$8 ? 5 ? 11 ? 4 = 6$$

230 Can you fit these numbers into the grid? One number has already been given to help you.

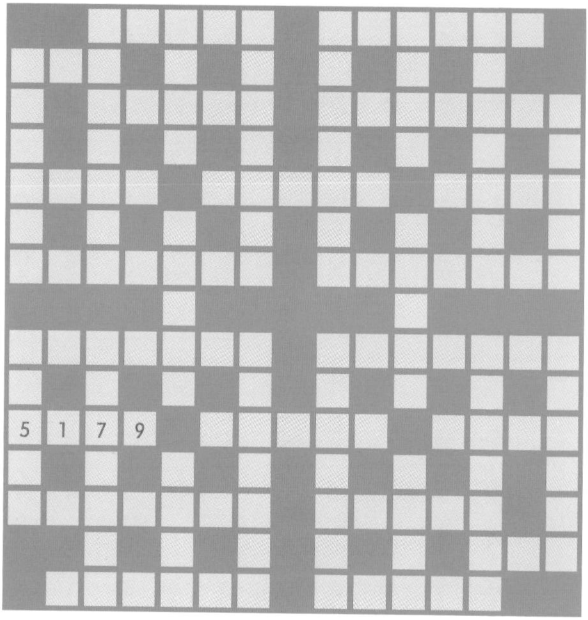

3 FIGURES

562
685

4 FIGURES

1562
2188
2463
3456
~~5179~~
8024
9247
9396

5 FIGURES

29875
35094
41668
51236
51503
54173
62262
72825
75128
93564

6 FIGURES

242613
690367
990383
997692

7 FIGURES

1660317
2035255
2551508
2678559
3283634
3459441

5025452
5620728
5661522
5840183
5926975
7387532
9275906
9720529

231 The number 9876569 appears just once in this number-search grid and occurs in a straight line, running either backward or forward in a horizontal, vertical or diagonal direction. Can you locate it?

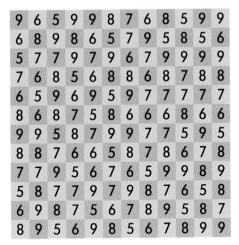

9	6	5	9	9	8	7	6	8	5	9	9
6	8	9	8	6	5	7	9	5	8	5	6
5	7	7	9	7	9	6	7	9	9	9	9
7	6	8	5	6	8	8	6	8	7	8	8
6	5	9	6	9	5	9	7	7	7	7	7
8	6	8	7	5	8	6	6	6	8	6	6
9	9	5	8	7	9	9	7	7	5	9	5
8	8	7	6	6	5	8	7	8	6	7	8
7	7	9	5	6	7	6	5	9	9	8	9
5	8	7	7	9	7	9	8	7	6	5	8
6	9	8	7	5	6	7	8	9	5	8	7
8	9	5	6	9	8	5	6	7	8	9	9

232 What is the value of the missing domino?

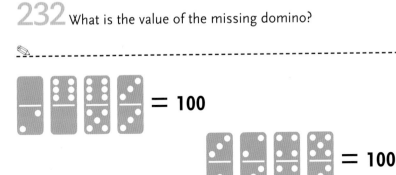

233 Place the jigsaw pieces into the square grid. Each row is identical to its corresponding column (e.g. the third row across = the third column down) in both the colors and numbers used.

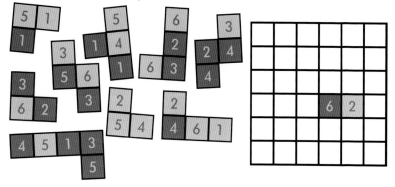

234 Every row and column contains the same numbers and symbols, but they are arranged in a different order each time. Find the correct order to arrive at the totals shown.

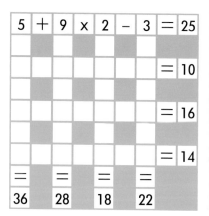

5	+	9	×	2	−	3	=	25
							=	10
							=	16
							=	14
=		=		=		=		
36		28		18		22		

235 Make a calculation that will equal 196 using some or all of the numbers in the circle with any of the four standard mathematical operations (+, -, x and ÷). Additional hint: There is an easy way of spotting the only solution!

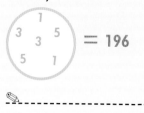

236 Which is the only four-figure number to appear twice in the jumble of numbers on the right?

✎ ---------------------

1534 2134 2143 3514 3124 4125
1253 2514 3154 4123 1342
3254 3214 1234 4132
4325 4321 3412 4352
4213 1243 3421 4231
3142 1324 2314 4531
3241 4123 4312 2341
1254 2351 1423 3452 2413
1235 2415 1432 2431

237 Can you place the 2, 3, 4 and 5 of each card suit so that every row and column (but not necessarily the diagonals) contains exactly one card of each denomination and suit?

			3♠
5♥			4♦
	4♣		
		2♦	

238 Given that scales A and B balance perfectly, how many stars are needed to balance scale C?

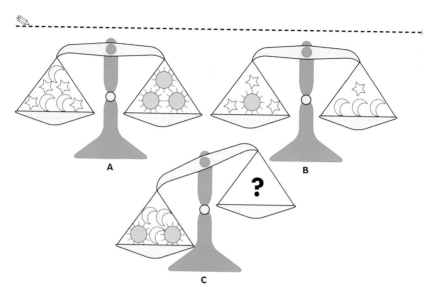

A   B

C

239 In this puzzle, each block is equal to the sum of the two numbers beneath it. Can you find the missing numbers (one of them is a negative number)?

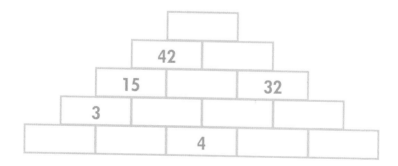

240 Place a number in the central box by which all the other numbers can be divided without leaving a remainder. The number is greater than 1.

426

497

355

?

284

142

568

241 What percentage of the shape below is shaded?

✎ ------------------------------

242 Which is the only five-figure number to appear twice in the jumble below?

✎ ------------------------------

95327 71492 19722 25497 22917 70915
39152 41597 29357 73912 98271
82157 21937 49127 71921
70215 72619 27891 76251
27051 90172 21719 73129
29371 92617 12970 75829
25179 16912 76291 12791
91577
81259 97182 71492 31792
91255 31795 97221 17209

243 Place the jigsaw pieces into the square grid so that each row, column and diagonal adds up to the same number. Furthermore, if you add the four corners, the middle four numbers, or each quadrant, each one totals that same number too!

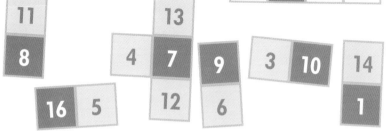

244 Can you divide the circle opposite into three equal parts, so that the numbers in every section add up to ten? No section should contain three or more identical digits and none should contain the same quantity of digits as any other.

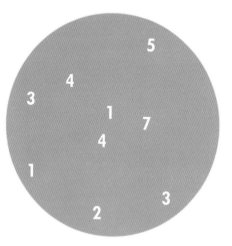

245 Mathematical wizards among you will be able to work out the answers to these equations using only pen and paper. But can you find them in the grid? They may be read up, down, backward, forward or diagonally.

1 77×7^2
2 555×123
3 $9^2 \times 9^2 \times 9^2$
4 $5^2 \times 6^2 \times 7^2$
5 $88,911 \times 5$
6 4^6
7 $10,017 \div 9$
8 $1234 + 5432$
9 $15,510 - 7755$
10 $12,012 - 4004 - 4004$

4	4	4	5	5	5
3	4	5	1	5	3
7	7	1	6	6	1
7	1	2	0	9	4
3	8	4	0	0	4
6	6	6	6	4	1

246 Which number will divide into all the other numbers without leaving a remainder? The number is greater than 1.

801

623

712

?

534

267

178

247 Can you fit these numbers into the grid? One number has already been inserted to help you get started.

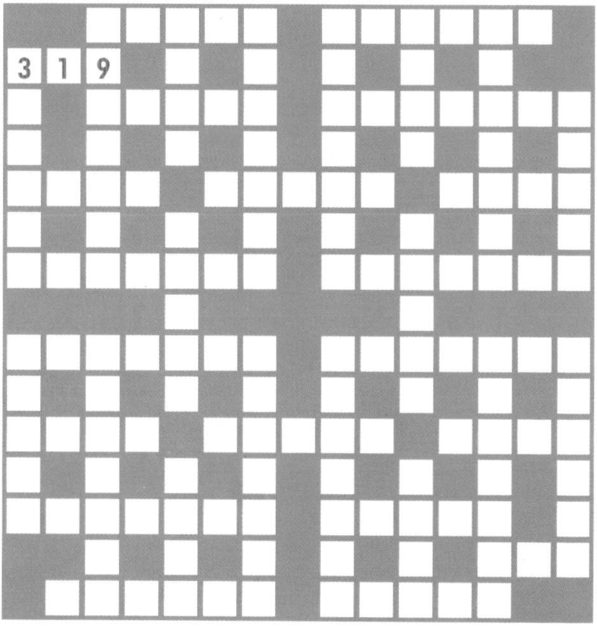

3 FIGURES
~~319~~
407

4 FIGURES
1815
3639
5782
6221
7404
8386
8650
9533

5 FIGURES
25284
41646
47624
53959
68496
71964
73101
76511
86033
97654

6 FIGURES
296620
319928
335947
827088

7 FIGURES
1063397
2381443
2981659
4920329
6149306
7320247
7532710
7882674
7909247
8053988
8177087
8320636
8790253
8794746

248 Given that scales A and B balance perfectly, how many bananas are needed to balance scale C?

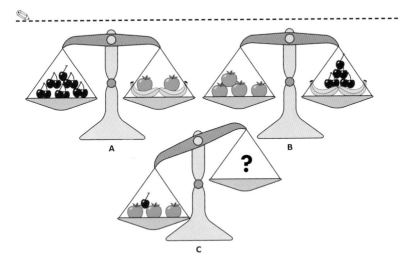

249 In this mathematical crossword every row and column contains the same numbers and signs, but they are arranged in a different order each time. Find the correct order to arrive at the final totals shown.

5	+	4	−	7	x	3	=	6
							=	25
							=	36
							=	30
=		=		=		=		
18		42		26		35		

250 What percentage of the shape below is shaded?

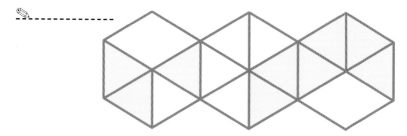

251 Each block is equal to the (positive) difference of the two numbers beneath it. The completed pyramid will contain the digits from 1 to 10, one number in each block. We have placed two of the numbers for you.

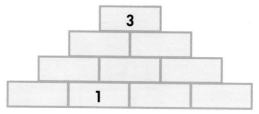

252 Place the jigsaw pieces into the hexagonal grid so that each straight line of cells (in any of three directions) always adds up to the same number.

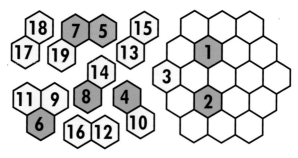

253 Can you work out how to fit all these numbers into the grid? One number has already been inserted to help you get started.

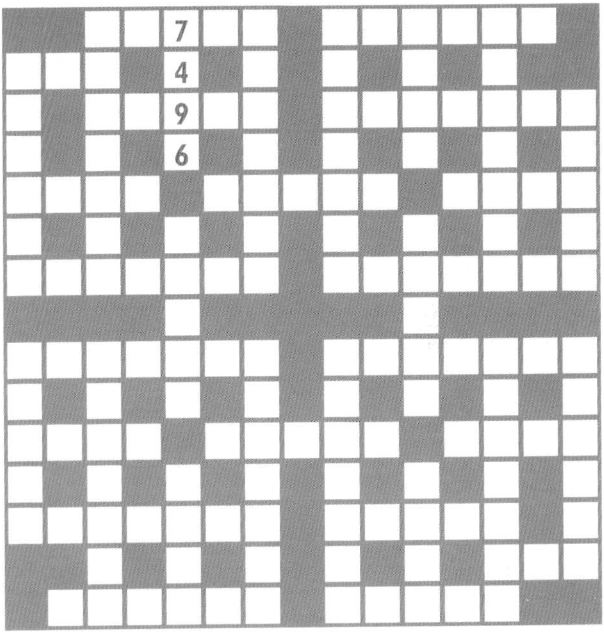

3 FIGURES

377
725

4 FIGURES

1343
2225
3478
5343
5753
6261
7073
~~7496~~

5 FIGURES

16575
31357
40564
75942
78291
79528
88136
94738
98088
99331

6 FIGURES

198977
745393
765509
806572

7 FIGURES

5248734
6970312
7373099
7375714
7466293
7610941
7952901

8023829
8150227
8591817
9268719
9576544
9945134
9949989

254 Make a calculation totaling the figure below using some or all of the numbers in the circle with any of the four standard mathematical operations (+, -, x and ÷).

✎ ------------------------------

= 910

255 Damian was born on September 10, 1973. Because of his birthday, he had a party to celebrate his life on January 26, 2001. Can you guess the significance of the party date?

✎ ----------------------

256 Each block is equal to the (positive) difference of the two numbers beneath it. The completed pyramid will contain the numbers from 1 to 15, with one number in each block. We have placed two of them for you.

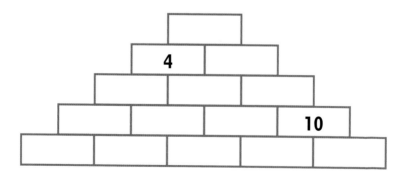

Sudoku & Kakuro Puzzles

Sudoku and Kakuro:
Today's Most Popular Brain Teasers!

SUDOKU

A standard Sudoku puzzle is made of a 9x9 grid, subdivided into 3x3 blocks, called regions. When you begin a puzzle, numbers are already filled into some of the 81 boxes in the puzzle. Your job is to fill in the remaining squares, following just one rule: Each of the numbers 1 through 9 must appear in each row, column and region. In other words, no row, column or region can have two of the same number.

Sudoku puzzles have difficulty ratings based on how many numbers are placed in boxes at the start. An easy puzzle might have 36 numbers already provided; a very hard puzzle might have just 24. No matter how hard or easy, though, Sudoku puzzles can always be solved through logic. That means there is never a point at which you are forced to guess. Each Sudoku has one unique solution.

KAKURO

Kakuro puzzles resemble crossword puzzles, but use numbers instead of words. The clues appear directly on the puzzle, in the blocked-out squares. The clues tell you the sum of the numbers in the column or row that lead from it (a clue in the top right of a square tells you the sum of the row to its right; a clue in the bottom left of a square tells you the sum of the column below it).

The rules for filling in squares are simple: You can only use the numbers 1 through 9, and the same number cannot appear twice in a combination. For example, if there is a two-square row and the clue says "4," the answer has to be 1-3 or 3-1, because 2-2 is not allowed. Likewise, a three-square row with a clue of "6" must be some variation of 1-2-3, since 4-1-1 violates the rule.

Kakuro puzzle grids can be any size, although usually the squares within them have to be arranged symmetrically. As a rule of thumb, the more blank squares a puzzle contains, the harder it is. Similarly, the more combinations a clue has, the harder it is to solve, so you should look for clues you know only have 1 or 2 combinations first.

1 Sudoku—Easy

	1		2			3	4	
		2			5			6
3				1	7	5		2
	3	8		2		4		
			1	4	3			
		9		8		7	2	
4		3	9	6				5
7			8			9		
	2	5			4		1	

2 Sudoku—Easy

	1	2	3			4	5	
		6		4	5		7	
		1					8	3
5	3			9		6		
			6	7	4			
		4		3			2	9
2	6				8			
	9		4	5		7		
	4	5			3	1	6	

3 Sudoku—Easy

	1	2		3	4		5	6
	7		2					
	8							
7	4	9		1		2	6	8
			7	4	2			
3	2	5		6		1	4	7
							7	
					9		8	
6	9		1	5		4	3	

4 Sudoku—Easy

		1	2					
	3			1	4		5	6
4	7							
8	4	6		5		3	9	2
			3	9	8			
5	9	3		6		1	8	7
							4	8
3	2		8	4		1		
				5	9			

5 Sudoku—Medium

		1			2		3	
		4			5	6		
	7		4			8	9	
	9	2		1				
	3			9				5
				4		7	6	
	5	9			7		4	
		7	3			1		
	6			8			9	

6 Sudoku—Medium

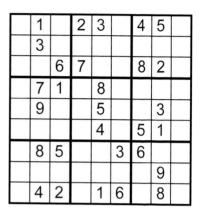

	1		2	3		4	5	
	3							
		6	7			8	2	
	7	1		8				
	9			5			3	
				4		5	1	
	8	5			3	6		
							9	
	4	2		1	6		8	

7 Sudoku—Medium

1					2	3	4	
5			3					
	6			4		7	8	
	3	9		6				
	2			9			1	
				8		4	5	
	8	6		3			9	
					9			2
	1	3	7					4

8 Sudoku—Medium

			1			2		
	3			4	5			6
			6	7		8	4	
	7	8		1				
	4			5			9	
				2		4	3	
	5	1		6	2			
9			7	8			5	
		6			3			

9 Sudoku—Hard

	1	2		3		4		
			5	6				7
3			8					
7				9				5
					2			6
9				7	3			
		8		4		1	2	

10 Sudoku—Hard

		1						
2				3	4	5		
			6					
5		7		2				
8				4				9
				8		6		4
					7			
		9	1	6				8
						3		

11 Sudoku—Hard

	1							2
				3				4
		5					6	
		2	1	6				
4				5				7
				7	8	9		
	7					5		
3				4				
9							8	

12 Sudoku—Hard

					1	2		
	3							
4		5		6				
		7	1		5			
8				4				3
			9		2	1		
				5		8		4
							6	
		9	7					

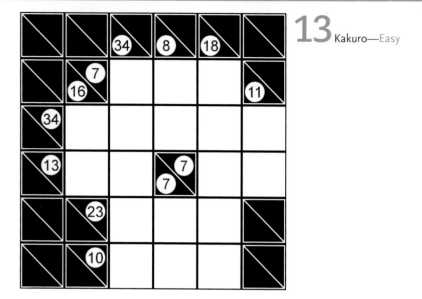

13 Kakuro—Easy

14 Kakuro—Easy

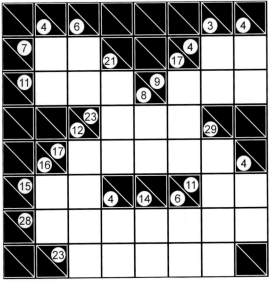

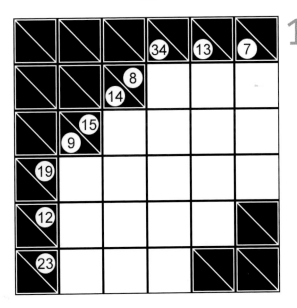

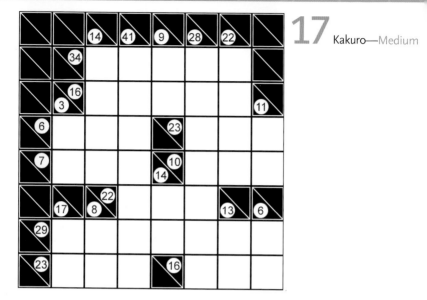

17 Kakuro—Medium

18 Kakuro—Medium

19 Kakuro—Medium

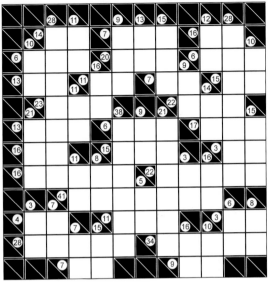

20 Kakuro—Medium

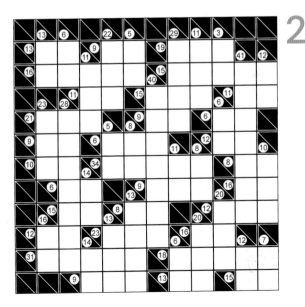

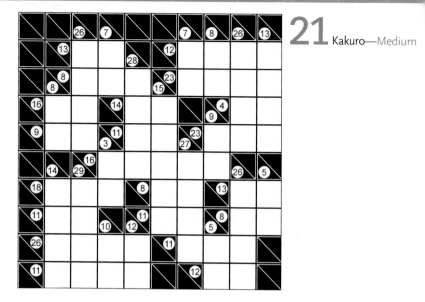

21 Kakuro—Medium

22 Kakuro—Hard

23 Kakuro—Hard

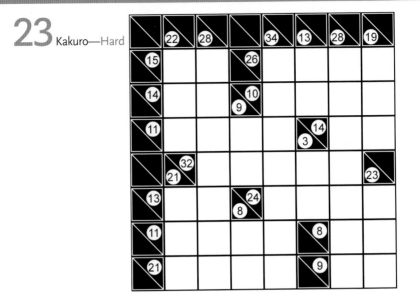

24 Kakuro—Hard

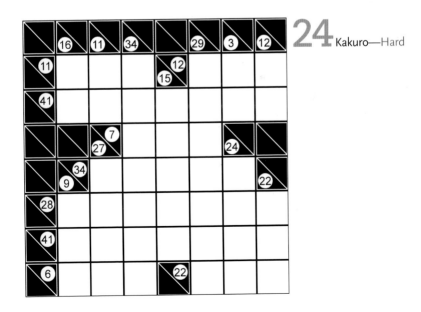

Answer key

Part One
Word Puzzles
PUZZLE 1

1 Church
2 Cheese
3 Seldom
4 Omega
5 Galleon
6 Once
7 Central
8 Allow

9 Owner
10 Erase
11 Sentence
12 Certain
13 Invisible
14 Leader
15 Errand

PUZZLE 2

The anagram is Argentina.

PUZZLE 3

PUZZLE 4

ACROSS

9 Remain (stay)
14 Large house (mansion)
5 Tug (pull)
21 Phobia (fear)
7 Plenty (ample)
2 School group (class)
15 Insect (moth)
11 Finished (done)
23 First appearance (debut)
6 Noisy (loud)
22 Shortly (soon)
18 Animal skin (pelt)
20 Stadium (arena)

DOWN

1 Corrosion (rust)
2 Stiff mud (clay)
19 Glance (look)
18 Beyond (past)
3 Snow vehicle (sled)
4 Wreck (ruin)
17 Difficult (hard)
8 Sea journey (passage)

16 Undo (open)
12 Small weight (ounce)
10 Allow in (admit)
9 Tempest (storm)
13 Build (erect)

PUZZLE 5

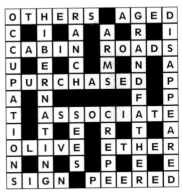

PUZZLE 6

The anagram is Shakespeare.

PUZZLE 7

	1	Broken	8	Eternal
	2	Enough	9	Altar
	3	Ghost	10	Arrive
	4	Stalemate	11	Venom
	5	Terrible	12	Omitted
	6	Lesson	13	Educate
	7	Onset	14	Teaspoon

PUZZLE 8

PUZZLE 9

1	Protest	8	Alarm
2	Strange	9	Mystery
3	Gemini	10	Yacht
4	Ignite	11	Trouble
5	Teacher	12	Leading
6	Reduce	13	Gallon
7	Cereal		

PUZZLE 10

ACROSS

9 Infant (child)
13 Between (through)
14 Fortunate (lucky)
1 Seashore (beach)
5 Join (connect)
15 Twelve (dozen)
3 Clutch (grasp)
11 Winch (hoist)
8 Weary (tired)
7 Weighty (heavy)

DOWN

5 Roman vehicle (chariot)
1 Turn red (blush)
6 Taint (tarnish)
10 Soiled (dirty)
3 Welcome (greet)
9 Christmas song (carol)
11 Hunting dog (hound)
4 Beg (plead)
2 Convenient (handy)
12 Teach (train)

PUZZLE 11

The anagram is Jingle Bells.

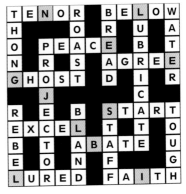

PUZZLE 12

PUZZLE 13

1 Macabre
2 Remain
3 Nadir
4 Robust
5 Stamina
6 Ancestry
7 Yield
8 Dismantle
9 Lethal
10 Altitude
11 Expand
12 Danger

PUZZLE 14

PUZZLE 15

PUZZLE 16

Ant (pageant and anthem).

PUZZLE 17

Botany.

PUZZLE 18

Brainwave is the only word in which a letter (a) is repeated.

PUZZLE 19

KERCA=creak.

PUZZLE 20

A Hot
B Hire
C Seedy
D Dream

E Exams
F Crowd
G Thoughts
H Approach

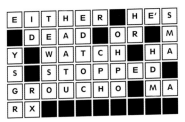

E	I	T	H	E	R			H	E'	S
		D	E	A	D		O	R		M
Y		W	A	T	C	H		H	A	
S		S	T	O	P	P	E	D		
G	R	O	U	C	H	O		M	A	
R	X									

PUZZLE 21

Possible answers include:

AIR
ALERT
ALIEN
ARE
ART
CERTAIN
CERTAINLY
ERA
ICE
ITALY
LATIN
LAY
LIE
LINE
LIT
NICE
NICELY
NICER
RAIL

RAIN
RAT
RAY
RECITAL
RELAY
RELY
RICE
TAIL
TALE
TAR
TIE
TILE
TIN
TIRE
TRAIL
TRAIN
TRAY
TRIAL

PUZZLE 22

1	P	E	R	M	I	T
2	O	R	N	A	T	E
3	P	A	L	A	C	E
4	U	M	P	I	R	E
5	L	A	T	E	L	Y
6	A	N	T	L	E	R
7	T	H	R	I	L	L
8	I	M	P	E	D	E
9	O	P	P	O	S	E
10	N	E	A	R	B	Y

PUZZLE 23

C	O	W	B	O	Y	S		R	E	S	T	O	R	E
H		E		L		P		A		I		P		N
O	I	L	E	D		I	N	C	O	R	R	E	C	T
K		L		E		R		E			R		E	
I	N	K		R	E	I	N	S		S	T	A	I	R
N		N				T				A				E
G	R	O	W	N		U	N	C	O	V	E	R	E	D
		W		A		A		U		E		E		
W	I	N	D	M	I	L	L	S		D	E	P	T	H
E				E				T			L		A	
I	D	E	A	S		C	H	O	I	R		A	I	R
G		R				L		M		A		C		N
H	U	R	R	I	C	A	N	E		D	R	I	V	E
T		O		N		P		R		I		N		S
S	H	R	I	N	K	S		S	P	O	N	G	E	S

PUZZLE 24

Large dish.

PUZZLE 25

Steady.

PUZZLE 26

WARM
WARD
CARD
CORD
COLD

PUZZLE 27

Double.

PUZZLE 28

14-letter word: cinematography.

PUZZLE 29

PUZZLE 30

Scientific equipment	APPARATUS
Blown spheres	BUBBLES
It preys on your mind	CONSCIENCE
United we stand, ___ we fall	DIVIDED
St. ___, U.S. hospital drama	ELSEWHERE
The golden anniversary	FIFTIETH
Swimmers wear them	GOGGLES
A vital statistic	HEIGHT
Type of police parade	IDENTIFICATION
A feeling of envy	JEALOUSY
Rap with the knuckles	KNOCK
Without exaggeration	LITERALLY
Embalmed body	MUMMY
A golfer's favorite hole?	NINETEENTH
The other side	OPPOSITION
Marionette	PUPPET
In a line, like its five vowels?	QUEUEING
Store of water	RESERVOIR
Don't run with them	SCISSORS
You go to a doctor for it	TREATMENT
That's odd	UNUSUAL
Clear in the memory	VIVID
Native American dwelling	WIGWAM
Charles Foster Kanes home	XANADU
The day before	YESTERDAY
Jagged line	ZIGZAG

PUZZLE 31

PUZZLE 32

R	A	Z	O	R		A		S	U	G	A	R
E		E		E	I	G	H	T		R		H
F	A	B	L	E		I		E	N	E	M	Y
E		R		D	E	N	S	E		E		M
R	O	A	D	S		G		R	A	N	G	E
	T		R					N		L		
W	H	E	A	T				A	G	A	I	N
	E		M					E		D		
T	R	E	A	T		W		U	R	G	E	D
O		M		I	D	E	A	S		R		I
W	I	P	E	D		A		I	T	E	M	S
E		T		A	P	R	O	N		A		K
L	O	Y	A	L		S		G	A	T	E	S

PUZZLE 33

NETDR=trend

PUZZLE 34

T I L E
I R I S
L I M P
E S P Y

PUZZLE 35

NEED
WEED

WEND

WAND

WANT

PUZZLE 36

The word is trigonometrical.

M
N O
T I C
T R I O
L A R G E

PUZZLE 37

PUZZLE 38

Attempt.

PUZZLE 39

Gain (bargain and gainsay).

PUZZLE 40

PUZZLE 41

Confectionary.

PUZZLE 42

IT
BIT
BITE
BITER
BITTER
BITTERN

PUZZLE 43

Sluggish.

PUZZLE 44

Hand (backhand and handsome).

PUZZLE 45

Isobar.

PUZZLE 46

Possible answers include:

AIM	HAM
CAMP	HIM
CAMPS	HIPS
CAP	HIS
CAPS	INCH
CHAIN	MAIN
CHAIN	MAP
CHAINS	MAPS
CHAMPIONS	PAIN
CHIMP	PAINS
CHIMPS	PIN
CHIN	PINCH
CHIP	PINS
CHIPS	SPAIN
COIN	SPIN
COINS	

PUZZLE 47

Lerdca=Cradle

PUZZLE 48

DINE
FINE
FIND
FEND
FEED

PUZZLE 49

SOS HELP
Read the missing letters between each of
the groups (e.g., "S" between the "R" and
"T" of SVQAR and TBCIN, etc.).

PUZZLE 50

Gang (chaingang and gangway).

PUZZLE 51

L	O	S	T
O	B	O	E
S	O	L	E
T	E	E	M

PUZZLE 52

S	T	U	N	S		E	N	J	O	Y	A	B	L	E
U		P		K		A		E		O		A		R
B	A	R	R	I	E	R		T	H	U	N	D	E	R
T		I				T				R		G		O
R	I	G	I	D		H	O	U	R	S		E	R	R
A		H		U				N				R		
C	U	T		C	O	U	R	T		T	A	S	T	Y
T				K		P		I		I				E
S	T	A	Y	S		S	T	E	E	R		W	A	S
		M				E				E		H		T
E	Y	E		A	T	T	I	C		D	R	O	V	E
X		R		S				A				E		R
T	H	I	C	K	E	R		R	E	M	O	V	E	D
R		C		E		A		E		U		E		A
A	B	A	N	D	O	N	E	D		M	E	R	C	Y

PUZZLE 53

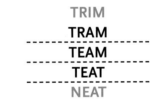

TRIM
TRAM
TEAM
TEAT
NEAT

PUZZLE 54

Semiprecious stone.

PUZZLE 55

1	C	H	A	N	C	E
2	A	T	T	I	R	E
3	L	E	S	S	O	N
4	C	A	N	Y	O	N
5	U	R	A	N	U	S
6	L	A	T	H	E	R
7	A	C	T	I	V	E
8	T	R	E	M	O	R
9	O	B	J	E	C	T
10	R	E	M	E	D	Y

PUZZLE 56

C	A	M	E
A	R	E	A
M	E	W	S
E	A	S	Y

PUZZLE 57

PUZZLE 58

Cardinal.

PUZZLE 59

PUZZLE 60

Navigation.

1	N O R M A L
2	A B L A Z E
3	V I S I O N
4	I N F A N T
5	G L O B A L
6	A R C H E R
7	T I M B E R
8	I G N O R E
9	O P T I O N
10	N E P H E W

PUZZLE 61

S A M E
A N E W
M E R E
E W E S

PUZZLE 62

The names are an anagram of Alice in Wonderland.

PUZZLE 63

```
L I F E N E L E F I L L L E
E N I L N I N L N N E I I L
N E I E F I L I N E F F F F
N N F E E E L F L L I E E E
E I L F I N E L I E F E L N
N E I I N I F F I N I L
I L I F E L I L E I L L N E
L I I E I E F N E L E E N F
E L I F E L I F L F F F E E
F E E I E I N E I N I N N
E F I L E F I L E F N L E F
L I I I E I I I N I E E L L
I L I F E L I N I L I F E L
N N I E F E E I L E L E N L
```

PUZZLE 64

Wronged. (All the others have the consecutive letters ONE embedded in them.)

PUZZLE 65

CANADA
BARBADOS
MOROCCO
TRINIDAD
VENEZUELA
FINLAND
HONG KONG
HUNGARY
INDIA
JORDAN
KENYA
FALKLAND
  ISLANDS
MYANMAR

NETHERLANDS
MONACO
PHILIPPINES
IRAQ
PERU
RUSSIA
TURKEY
URUGUAY
VIETNAM
WALES
MEXICO
ITALY
BRAZIL

PUZZLE 66

Hand (stagehand and handsome)

PUZZLE 67

Place your negative in locker 40 at Sydney Opera House by Tuesday
(Read the words phonetically.)

PUZZLE 68

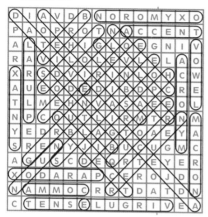

PUZZLE 69

PUZZLE 70

A river.

PUZZLE 71

Mongoose.

PUZZLE 72

1 Joker
2 Rajah
3 Hertz
4 Above
5 Avert

PUZZLE 73

Espousal, adoption.

PUZZLE 74

A DOZEN
B HARK
C ODE
D FLOWER
E SEWER
F TAX
G ANSWER
H DISCUSS
I TOWEL
J EBBING
K RETICENTLY

Author's name: D. HOFSTADTER.

PUZZLE 75

Boastful coward.

PUZZLE 76

Australian animal.

PUZZLE 77

Handle (manhandle and handlebars)

PUZZLE 78

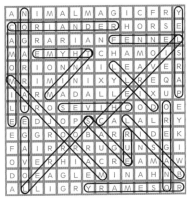

PUZZLE 79

PUZZLE 80

Lower.

PUZZLE 81

Flighty.

PUZZLE 82

1	C	H	U	R	C	H
2	O	B	T	A	I	N
3	N	O	V	I	C	E
4	F	I	N	I	S	H
5	E	X	C	I	T	E
6	R	E	D	U	C	E
7	E	L	A	P	S	E
8	N	I	M	B	L	E
9	C	H	A	N	C	E
10	E	S	C	O	R	T

Part Two
Memory &
Visual Puzzles

PUZZLE 83

D.

PUZZLE 84

44% is yellow, 56% is white.

PUZZLE 85

A. The square in the middle goes to the top of the pyramid. The remaining two squares remain at the bottom but switch places.

PUZZLE 86

B. There are three types of arrows being repeated in sequence. Every second arrow points upward.

PUZZLE 87

PUZZLE 88

One solution is as follows:

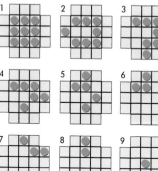

PUZZLE 89

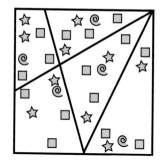

PUZZLE 90

Cube D.

PUZZLE 91

40. Each dice has a total of 21 spots. We can see 23 spots, so there are 63 - 23 = 40 hidden from view.

PUZZLE 92

One-third is shaded.

PUZZLE 93

PUZZLE 94

B. Each line has a green, a black and a white outer circle; a green, a black and a white middle circle; and a small black and a small white inner circle (with one shape having no inner circle). The missing shape must therefore have a green outer circle, a green middle circle (since no other middle circles are showing in the third row it follows that the first must be black and the second white) and no inner circle, hence B.

PUZZLE 95

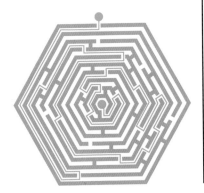

PUZZLE 96

1. Triangle
2. Pentagon
3. Three
4. Eight
5. Four
6. Nine
7. Circle
8. 19

PUZZLE 97

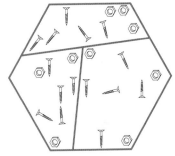

PUZZLE 98

C. The dot moves one corner clockwise at each stage, while the circle moves two places counterclockwise.

PUZZLE 99

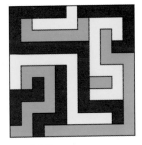

PUZZLE 100

5 revolutions. Find the lowest common multiple of all the numbers (in this case 140), then divide that number by the number of teeth in the largest cog to get the number of revolutions, in this case 5.

PUZZLE 101

The missing domino is B—they all have even numbers of spots.

PUZZLE 102

Here's one possible solution:

PUZZLE 103

Cube A.

PUZZLE 104

C is different because the visible spots on two adjacent sides add up to 7. On all standard dice, the spots on opposite sides add up to 7.

PUZZLE 105

91. $(1^2 + 2^2 + 3^2 + 4^2 + 5^2 + 6^2)$.

PUZZLE 106

A. In each case the sequence contains a black and a blue circle, and a black and a blue square. These move about at random.

PUZZLE 107

D. The bright yellow circle moves 90° clockwise, while the darker yellow circle moves 135° clockwise.

PUZZLE 108

The whole puzzle is the odd one out. The letters are an anagram of OUTSIDER, a synonym for misfit or odd one out.

PUZZLE 109

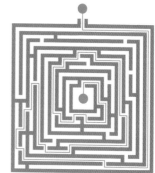

PUZZLE 110

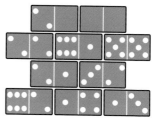

PUZZLE 111

D and G, thus:

PUZZLE 112

F is the odd one out, since each of the blue segments moves one space clockwise of the previously lettered arrangement, but the blue segments on F move one space counterclockwise of the arrangement on A.

PUZZLE 113

I will be at the chalet.
The number indicates the position of the
letter in the word "white" or "black". So,
for example, a "3" in a white circle is the
letter "i", a "1" in a white circle is the letter
"w", etc., giving the answer.

PUZZLE 114

The value of the missing domino is 0-0.
The total number of spots on every
domino is the value of the total numbers
of spots on the two dominoes immediately
beneath it.

PUZZLE 115

A and F are identical.

PUZZLE 116

27

PUZZLE 117

Cube D.

PUZZLE 118

Blue, orange and yellow. Each group of
four triangles:

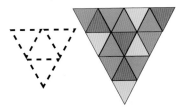

contains one of each of the colors.

PUZZLE 119

41. There are 21 dots on each die, thus a
total of 63 dots on the three dice. Since 22
dots are visible, the total number of dots on
the sides that are not visible amounts to 41.

PUZZLE 120

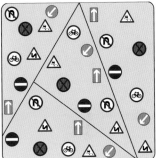

PUZZLE 121

B. Each line contains one
circle, one square and one
triangle. Each line contains a yellow star, a
white star and no star. Each line contains a
green symbol, an orange symbol and a
purple symbol. The missing symbol must
be a purple circle containing a yellow star.

PUZZLE 122

Cube B.

PUZZLE 123

PUZZLE 124

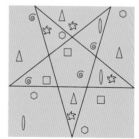

B. Each line contains two orange frames and a yellow frame. Each line contains two orange crosses and a yellow cross. Each line contains an orange circle, a yellow circle and no circle. The missing picture must have an orange frame, with a yellow cross and a yellow circle.

PUZZLE 125

C. The square originally on the left rotates 90° clockwise and moves to bottom right, the square originally on the right rotates 90° clockwise and moves to bottom left, and the square in the middle rotates 180° and moves to the top of the pyramid.

PUZZLE 126

PUZZLE 127

Cube A.

PUZZLE 128

PUZZLE 129

B and C are the same.

PUZZLE 130

Cube D.

PUZZLE 131

B. Each line contains two bikes facing left and one facing right. Each line contains two bells. Each line contains two horizontal pedals. The missing picture must be a bike facing right, with horizontal pedals and a bell.

PUZZLE 132

B. Triangles turn to circles and vice versa. Blue shapes turn to white and vice versa. Any triangles or circles outside the pentagon transfer to inside the pentagon and vice versa.

PUZZLE 133

C. The dots in the upper part of each domino increase in number by two every time, while those in the lower part decrease by one every time, thus the total number of dots on each domino rises by one every time.

PUZZLE 134

B. Each successive clock gains 4 hours 52 1/2 minutes.

PUZZLE 135

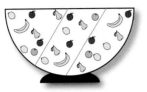

PUZZLE 136

PUZZLE 137

This is one possible solution.

PUZZLE 138

This is one possible solution.

PUZZLE 139

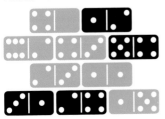

PUZZLE 140

A. Each large circle should appear three times, in each of three different colors, as should each star, each square and each small circle. So the missing shapes are a large white circle, a white star, a black square and a small white circle.

PUZZLE 141

C and D.

PUZZLE 142

B and E.

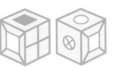

PUZZLE 143

Blue. Starting at the top left circle, every third circle reading left to right, row after row, is blue.

PUZZLE 144

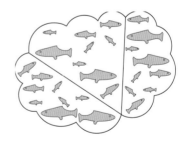

PUZZLE 145

B is the odd one out. E is a reflection of A, F of D and G of C.

PUZZLE 146

PUZZLE 147

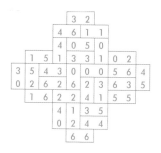

PUZZLE 148

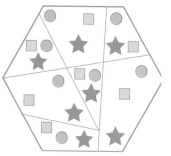

PUZZLE 149

The correct order is 4, 8, 1, 5, 3, 7, 2, 9, 6.
The fish ate his keys.

PUZZLE 150

B and C.

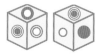

PUZZLE 151

Three moves. Each pair of coins is turned
180° when being moved.

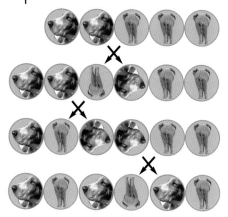

Part Three
Number Puzzles

PUZZLE 152

		111		
	49		62	
23		26		36
14	9		17	19

PUZZLE 153

1 2227	7 70,002
2 20,000	8 10,101
3 1066	9 3223
4 250,000	10 5555
5 5432	11 757
6 272,727	

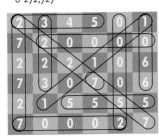

PUZZLE 154

PUZZLE 155

3798. All the others have all their numbers in ascending order.

PUZZLE 156

30 months.
Rocket A travels 360 ÷ 15 = 24 degrees around the circle every month.
Rocket B travels 360 ÷ 12 = 30 degrees around the circle every month.
Hence, B gains on A by 30 - 24 = 6 degrees every month. There are 180 degrees separating them at the beginning, so it will take 180 ÷ 6 = 30 months (or 2 1/2 years) before they crash.

PUZZLE 157

28 horses. Divide 168 by 6 (legs on horses = 4, legs on riders = 2) = 28.

PUZZLE 158

7.

PUZZLE 159

A, B and D.

PUZZLE 160

1	3	5	9	7	9	3	1	7	5	3	1
3	9	5	3	1	5	7	9	3	1	5	9
5	1	7	1	1	1	3	5	9	7	1	7
3	5	1	3	5	9	7	1	5	9	3	5
9	7	5	3	**9**	7	1	3	9	3	5	1
1	9	3	5	**7**	9	1	5	3	7	9	3
9	3	7	9	**5**	1	3	9	1	3	7	5
5	5	9	5	**3**	7	5	1	9	1	5	9
7	9	5	7	**1**	3	9	7	5	9	1	7
9	7	3	1	7	9	5	3	1	5	7	9
9	7	1	1	3	5	1	1	3	7	9	1
9	7	5	9	7	9	5	3	1	9	5	9

PUZZLE 161

33 + 12 ÷ 3 x 10 - 7 = 143

PUZZLE 162

19.

PUZZLE 163

28 ÷ 7 x 3 + 5 = 17

PUZZLE 164

4. Each circle has a value of 2, each star a value of 3 and each triangle a value of 5, so four stars are needed to balance scale C.
2. Each star has a value of 1, each triangle a value of 3 and each circle a value of 6, so two circles are needed to balance scale C.

PUZZLE 165

35 minutes.

PUZZLE 166

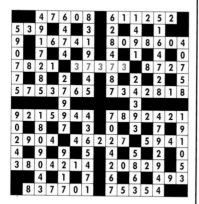

PUZZLE 167

In a 3 x 3 magic square, the central number is always one third of the magic number. Given that the central number was 3, the magic number (i.e., the number to which each row, column and diagonal must add up) must be 9. From here, it's easy to work out. Note the negative number in the right-hand column.

PUZZLE 168

9 (each clock is set 1 hour 40 minutes earlier than the last one).

PUZZLE 169

387. All the others can be paired off as they use the same three digits: 384/843, 481/148, 794/479, 296/926.

PUZZLE 170

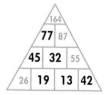

PUZZLE 171

Each consonant has a value of 6 and each vowel a value of 7, so England = 44.

PUZZLE 172

1080°. It can be worked out thus: divide the octagon into 8 triangles. In each the middle angle is 45°. The other two angles must then equal 135°. 135° x 8 = 1080°.

PUZZLE 173

35 + 7 ÷ 14 + 4 = 7

PUZZLE 174

84 months (or 7 years). This is because 84 is the lowest common multiple of 6 and 28—i.e., the lowest number that both 6 and 28 divide into without remainder.

PUZZLE 175

75 - 12 ÷ 7 x 22 + 2 = 200

PUZZLE 176

7	+	1	x	3	–	4	=	20
+		+		–		x		
4	x	3	–	1	+	7	=	18
x		x		x		–		
1	+	7	–	4	x	3	=	12
–		–		+		+		
3	x	4	–	7	+	1	=	6
=		=		=		=		
8		24		15		26		

PUZZLE 177

4. There are two alternating sequences: 10, 8, 6, 4 and 1, 3, 5, etc.

PUZZLE 178

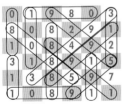

1	1089
2	1998
3	3125
4	191
5	1980
6	39483
7	5929

8	88888
9	995
10	113
11	5808
12	180
13	1001

PUZZLE 179

1	Degrees in three right angles	270
2	Years of marriage for a diamond anniversary	60
3	Isotope of uranium used in an atomic bomb	235
4	Minutes in a day	1440
5	Cost of the utility spaces in Monopoly	150
6	Number of the White House on Pennsylvania Avenue	1600
7	Age to which Methuselah lived	969
8	Number for a hurricane on the Beaufort Scale	12
9	Minutes of sound held on a standard CD	74
10	Chromosomes of a human being	46

PUZZLE 180

The total number of spots on each domino increases in value by three each time, thus C is missing.

PUZZLE 181

PUZZLE 182

PUZZLE 183

2. Look at the numbers formed by the diagonals of the other two, 19 x 2 = 38, 12 x 2 = 24, 16 x 2 = 32

PUZZLE 184

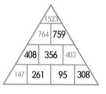

PUZZLE 185

8. The number of the minute hand is twice that of the hour hand in each case.

PUZZLE 186

76304. In all the others the number formed by the last three digits is the number formed by the first two digits multiplied by 3. In 76304, 76 x 4 = 304.

PUZZLE 187

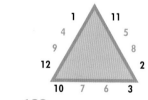

1   11
4   5
9   8
12   2
10 7 6 3

PUZZLE 188

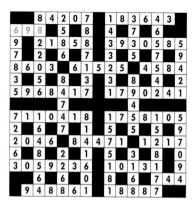

PUZZLE 189

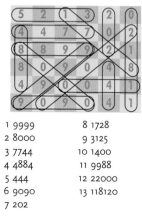

1 9999
2 8000
3 7744
4 4884
5 444
6 9090
7 202
8 1728
9 3125
10 1400
11 9988
12 22000
13 118120

PUZZLE 190

8 + 3 x 2 - 5 = 17
8 x 3 ÷ 2 + 5 = 17

PUZZLE 191

You can solve this by trial and error, but the mathematical way goes like this: let the missing number be "x". Filling in the rest of the pyramid (see illustration) means that the top number must equal
2x + 21.
We know this is equal to 67, hence 2x = 67 - 21 = 46,
so x = 23.

PUZZLE 192

x = 1m

PUZZLE 193

9. The total of each clock's hands follows the sequence 5, 10, 15, 20.

PUZZLE 194

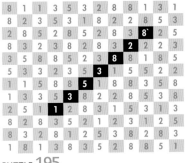

PUZZLE 195

(10 x 7 x 5) + 9 = 359.

PUZZLE 196

Looking from top to bottom, 7 and 4. In each hexagon, starting in the top right section, pairs of numbers total the same. In the first hexagon they total 12, in the second 15, and in the third 18. So, 6 + 12, 14 + 4 and 11 + 7 all total 18.

PUZZLE 197

1 Seconds in November (2,592,000). There are 1,609,344 millimeters in a mile.
2 22,500
3 12
4 177 (20 + 144 + 13)
5 -2
6 4 years ago
7 1, 2, 3
8 2 (half a rabbit can't eat anything!)

PUZZLE 198

PUZZLE 199

In a 3 x 3 magic square, the central number is always one-third of the magic number. Given that the magic number is 17, the central number must be 17 ÷ 3. From here, it's easy to fill out the rest.

10	2/3	19/3
2	17/3	28/3
5	32/3	4/3

PUZZLE 200

PUZZLE 201

1337. Multiply each number by 3 and subtract 1.

PUZZLE 202

17.

PUZZLE 203

22 1/2 months. In this time, A will have performed 3 3/4 orbits, while B will have done 1 1/2 orbits.

PUZZLE 204

177. The sequence is:
+1, -2, x3, ÷4, then repeat.

PUZZLE 205

12. Take (a + b + c) and subtract (d + e + f) to get the number in the middle.

(6 + 17 + 10) =	33
- (15 + 9 + 2) =	26
	7
(2 + 12 + 11) =	25
- (3 + 3 + 6) =	12
	13
(7 + 8 + 9) =	24
- (2 + 9 + 1) =	12
	12

PUZZLE 206

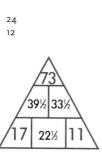

PUZZLE 207

From the diagram, we can see that 10 = 3 + 2X + Y, so 7 = 2X + Y. Also, 18 = 7 + X + 2Y, so 11 = X + 2Y. Adding those two equations together, we get 18 = 3X + 3Y, so 6 = X + Y. From the pyramid, the central block on row 2 is X + Y, so 6. Therefore Y + 7 = 12, so Y = 5, therefore X = 1. It is now easy to fill in the rest of the pyramid.

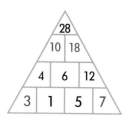

PUZZLE 208

PUZZLE 209

13.

PUZZLE 210

32% is green. 68% is white.
(Work it out by dividing the shape into 17 white triangles and 8 green: 8 of the total 25 are green = 32%.)

PUZZLE 211

23.

PUZZLE 212

Number 11. Work it out as follows:

	Odd	Even	Prime	Square	Straight line	Double Digits
1	✓			✓	✓	
2		✓	✓			
3	✓		✓			
4		✓		✓	✓	
5	✓		✓			
6		✓				
7	✓		✓		✓	
8		✓				
9	✓			✓		
10		✓				✓
11	✓		✓		✓	✓
12		✓				✓
13	✓		✓			✓
14		✓			✓	✓
15	✓					✓
16		✓		✓		✓

Only one number has four checks (four truths), and that is number 11.

PUZZLE 213

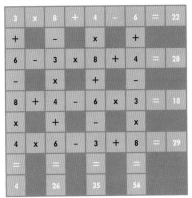

PUZZLE 214

One. Each knife has a value of 1, each spoon a value of 2 and each fork a value of 4, so one fork is needed to balance scale C.

PUZZLE 215

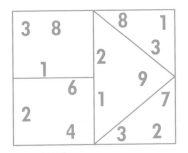

PUZZLE 216

3964. In all the others, the first digit multiplied by the third digit produces the number formed by the second and fourth digits, for example, 6472, where 6 x 7 = 42.

PUZZLE 217

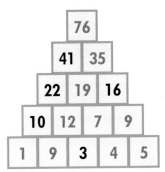

PUZZLE 218

10.
Work it out as follows:
x = correct solutions
y = incorrect solutions
then
x + y = 26
and
8x - 5y = 0
y = (26 - x)
8x - 5 (26 - x) = 0
8x = 130 - 5x
13x = 130
x = 10.

PUZZLE 219

(10 x 8 x 3) + 75 + 6 = 321
There are 25 other possible solutions.

PUZZLE 220

Clock C. Clocks A, B and D are the same but rotated. Clock C looks similar but has been flipped over (reflected).

PUZZLE 221

60 revolutions. Find the lowest common multiple, i.e. the smallest number into which all the numbers of cog teeth can be divided. The answer is this number divided by the number of teeth on the largest cog.

17 = 1 x 17
12 = 2 x 2 x 3
5 = (1) x 5
4 = (2 x 2)

To find the lowest common multiple, list all the prime factors of each number eliminating prime factors which are duplicated (shown in the brackets above). This leaves 1020, 1 x 17 x 2 x 2 x 3 x 5, which is the lowest number into which 17, 12, 5 and 4 can all be divided. Divide 1020 by 17 for the answer = 60.

PUZZLE 222

PUZZLE 223

PUZZLE 224

12. The missing domino is 6/6—add the total dots of the first and second dominoes and then multiply both by the third domino.

PUZZLE 225

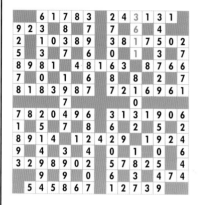

PUZZLE 226

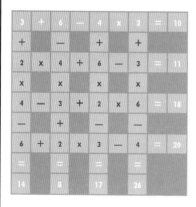

PUZZLE 227

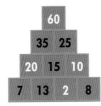

	60	
35	25	

| 20 | 15 | 10 |

| 7 | 13 | 2 | 8 |

PUZZLE 228

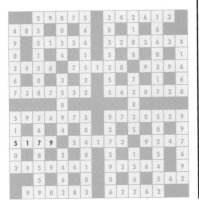

5	4	6	3	5	9	1	6	5	9	1	3
4	6	3	5	9	1	9	5	3	4	5	6
3	4	6	1	6	6	5	9	5	6	4	5
6	**5**	1	9	4	5	6	4	6	3	9	5
5	**4**	1	9	1	4	3	6	5	9	1	5
9	**3**	4	6	5	9	5	9	4	9	9	4
4	**6**	1	4	9	1	5	1	3	1	5	6
6	**5**	9	5	3	1	3	4	5	3	6	3
1	**9**	5	3	6	4	5	9	6	9	3	5
5	**1**	6	1	4	9	1	5	9	3	6	9
9	1	3	5	6	3	4	9	1	6	4	1
1	9	4	3	5	6	5	1	9	1	5	5

PUZZLE 229

$(8 + 5 + 11) \div 4 = 6$
$8 + 5 - 11 + 4 = 6$

PUZZLE 230

PUZZLE 231

9	6	5	9	9	8	7	6	8	5	9	9
6	8	9	8	6	5	7	9	5	8	5	6
5	7	7	**9**	7	9	6	7	9	9	9	9
7	6	8	5	**6**	8	8	6	8	7	8	8
6	5	9	6	9	**5**	9	7	7	7	7	7
8	6	8	7	5	8	**6**	6	6	8	6	6
9	9	5	8	7	9	9	**7**	7	5	9	5
8	8	7	6	6	5	8	7	**8**	6	7	8
7	7	9	5	6	7	6	5	**9**	**9**	8	9
5	8	7	7	9	7	9	8	7	6	5	8
6	9	8	7	5	6	7	8	9	5	8	7
8	9	5	6	9	8	5	6	7	8	9	9

PUZZLE 232

The missing domino is 0/1—add the total spots of the dominoes and multiply the answer by four.

PUZZLE 233

2	4	5	1	3	6
4	6	1	3	5	2
5	1	2	4	6	3
1	3	4	6	2	5
3	5	6	2	1	4
6	2	3	5	4	1

PUZZLE 234

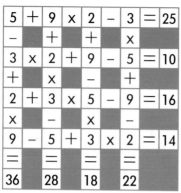

5	+	9	x	2	–	3	=	25
–		+		+		x		
3	x	2	+	9	–	5	=	10
+		x		–		+		
2	+	3	x	5	–	9	=	16
x		–		x		–		
9	–	5	+	3	x	2	=	14
=		=		=		=		
36		28		18		22		

PUZZLE 235

If you note that 196 is 14 squared, the solution is obvious:
((5 x 3) - 1) x ((5 x 3) - 1) = 196.

PUZZLE 236

4123.

PUZZLE 237

2♣	5♦	4♥	3♠
5♥	2♠	3♣	4♦
3♦	4♣	5♠	2♥
4♠	3♥	2♦	5♣

PUZZLE 238

11. Three stars weigh as much as one sun; and three moons weigh as much as five stars. Thus 11 stars are needed to balance scale C.

PUZZLE 239

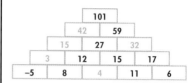

PUZZLE 240

71.

PUZZLE 241

37.5%.

PUZZLE 242

71492 appears twice.

PUZZLE 243

Each section totals 34.

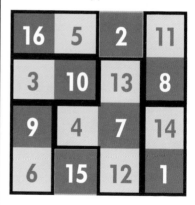

PUZZLE 244

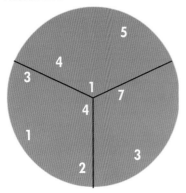

PUZZLE 245

1 3773	6 4096
2 68,265	7 1113
3 531,441	8 6666
4 44,100	9 7755
5 444,555	10 4004

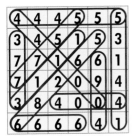

PUZZLE 246

89.

PUZZLE 247

	4	1	6	4	6		8	2	7	0	8	8	
3	1	9		2		1	1		4		3		
1		2	5	2	8	4		7	9	0	9	2	4	7
9		0		1		9	7		4		0		1
9	5	3	3		7	3	1	0	1		3	6	3	9
2		2		4		0		8		6		3		6
8	7	9	4	7	4	6		7	8	8	2	6	7	4
			6						4				
7	3	2	0	2	4	7		8	7	9	0	2	5	3
6		9		4		5		0		6		3		3
5	7	8	2		5	3	9	5	9		1	8	1	5
1		1		8		2		3		8		1		9
1	0	6	3	3	9	7		9	7	6	5	4		4
	5		8		1		8		5		4	0	7	
	2	9	6	6	2	0		8	6	0	3	3		

PUZZLE 248

4. One apple weighs as much as three cherries; and two bananas weigh as much as five cherries. Thus four bananas are needed to balance scale C.

PUZZLE 249

5	+	4	−	7	x	3	=	6
x		+		x		+		
3	+	5	x	4	−	7	=	25
+		−				x		
7	−	3	+	5	x	4	=	36
−		x		+		−		
4	x	7	−	3	+	5	=	30
=		=		=		=		
18		42		26		35		

PUZZLE 250

50%

PUZZLE 251

One possible solution is:

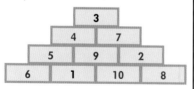

PUZZLE 252

Each line adds up to 38.

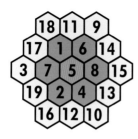

PUZZLE 253

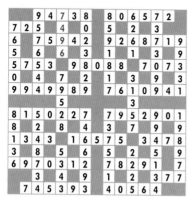

PUZZLE 254

$(8 + 5) \times 7 \times (6 + 4) = 910$.
There are 13 other possible solutions.

PUZZLE 255

It was the 10,000th day of Damian's life.

PUZZLE 256

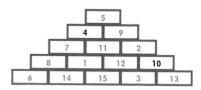

Part Four
Sudoku &
Kakuro Puzzles

PUZZLE 1

5	1	6	2	9	8	3	4	7
8	7	2	4	3	5	1	9	6
3	9	4	6	1	7	5	8	2
6	3	8	7	2	9	4	5	1
2	5	7	1	4	3	8	6	9
1	4	9	5	8	6	7	2	3
4	8	3	9	6	1	2	7	5
7	6	1	8	5	2	9	3	4
9	2	5	3	7	4	6	1	8

PUZZLE 3

9	1	2	8	3	4	7	5	6
5	7	3	2	9	6	8	1	4
4	8	6	5	7	1	3	2	9
7	4	9	3	1	5	2	6	8
8	6	1	7	4	2	5	9	3
3	2	5	9	6	8	1	4	7
2	5	4	6	8	3	9	7	1
1	3	7	4	2	9	6	8	5
6	9	8	1	5	7	4	3	2

PUZZLE 2

9	1	2	3	8	7	4	5	6
3	8	6	2	4	5	9	7	1
4	5	7	1	6	9	2	8	3
5	3	1	8	9	2	6	4	7
8	2	9	6	7	4	3	1	5
6	7	4	5	3	1	8	2	9
2	6	3	7	1	8	5	9	4
1	9	8	4	5	6	7	3	2
7	4	5	9	2	3	1	6	8

PUZZLE 4

6	5	1	2	8	7	4	3	9
2	3	8	9	1	4	7	5	6
4	7	9	5	3	6	8	2	1
8	4	6	7	5	1	3	9	2
7	1	2	3	9	8	5	6	4
5	9	3	4	6	2	1	8	7
9	6	5	1	7	3	2	4	8
3	2	7	8	4	9	6	1	5
1	8	4	6	2	5	9	7	3

PUZZLE 5

9	8	1	6	7	2	5	3	4
3	2	4	9	8	5	6	1	7
6	7	5	4	3	1	8	9	2
7	9	2	5	1	6	4	8	3
4	3	6	7	9	8	2	5	1
5	1	8	2	4	3	7	6	9
2	5	9	1	6	7	3	4	8
8	4	7	3	5	9	1	2	6
1	6	3	8	2	4	9	7	5

PUZZLE 7

1	9	7	8	5	2	3	4	6
5	4	8	3	7	6	9	2	1
3	6	2	9	4	1	7	8	5
4	3	9	1	6	5	2	7	8
8	2	5	4	9	7	6	1	3
6	7	1	2	8	3	4	5	9
2	8	6	5	3	4	1	9	7
7	5	4	6	1	9	8	3	2
9	1	3	7	2	8	5	6	4

PUZZLE 6

7	1	9	2	3	8	4	5	6
2	3	8	4	6	5	9	7	1
4	5	6	7	9	1	8	2	3
5	7	1	3	8	9	2	6	4
6	9	4	1	5	2	7	3	8
8	2	3	6	4	7	5	1	9
1	8	5	9	7	3	6	4	2
3	6	7	8	2	4	1	9	5
9	4	2	5	1	6	3	8	7

PUZZLE 8

6	9	4	1	3	8	2	7	5
8	3	7	2	4	5	9	1	6
2	1	5	6	7	9	8	4	3
3	7	8	9	1	4	5	6	2
1	4	2	3	5	6	7	9	8
5	6	9	8	2	7	4	3	1
7	5	1	4	6	2	3	8	9
9	2	3	7	8	1	6	5	4
4	8	6	5	9	3	1	2	7

PUZZLE 9

6	1	2	7	3	8	4	5	9
8	5	7	9	2	4	6	3	1
4	9	3	5	6	1	2	8	7
3	6	5	8	1	7	9	4	2
7	2	4	3	9	6	8	1	5
1	8	9	4	5	2	3	7	6
9	4	1	2	7	3	5	6	8
2	3	6	1	8	5	7	9	4
5	7	8	6	4	9	1	2	3

PUZZLE 11

6	1	3	5	8	4	7	9	2
8	9	7	2	3	6	1	5	4
2	4	5	7	9	1	3	6	8
7	8	2	1	6	9	4	3	5
4	6	9	3	5	2	8	1	7
5	3	1	4	7	8	9	2	6
1	7	6	8	2	3	5	4	9
3	2	8	9	4	5	6	7	1
9	5	4	6	1	7	2	8	3

PUZZLE 10

4	3	1	5	7	9	8	6	2
2	7	6	8	3	4	5	9	1
9	8	5	6	1	2	4	3	7
5	4	7	9	2	6	1	8	3
8	6	2	3	4	1	7	5	9
1	9	3	7	8	5	6	2	4
3	2	8	4	5	7	9	1	6
7	5	9	1	6	3	2	4	8
6	1	4	2	9	8	3	7	5

PUZZLE 12

9	8	6	3	7	1	2	4	5
7	3	1	5	2	4	6	8	9
4	2	5	8	6	9	3	1	7
3	9	7	1	8	5	4	2	6
8	1	2	6	4	7	9	5	3
5	6	4	9	3	2	1	7	8
1	7	3	2	5	6	8	9	4
2	5	8	4	9	3	7	6	1
6	4	9	7	1	8	5	3	2

PUZZLE 13

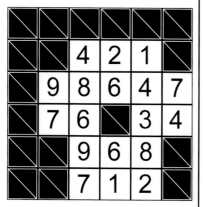

PUZZLE 15

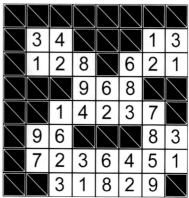

PUZZLE 14

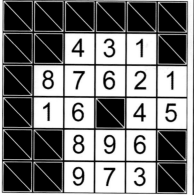

PUZZLE 16

PUZZLE 17

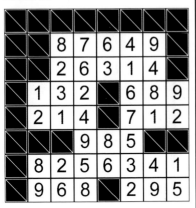

PUZZLE 18

PUZZLE 19

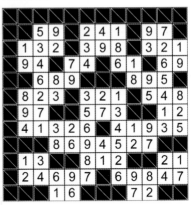

PUZZLE 20

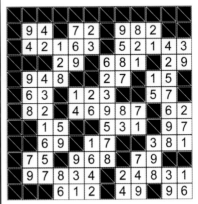

PUZZLE 21

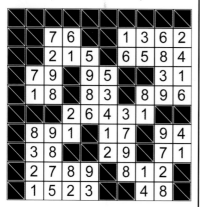

PUZZLE 23

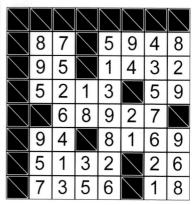

PUZZLE 22

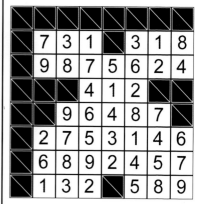

PUZZLE 24

	7	3	1		3	1	8
	9	8	7	5	6	2	4
		4	1	2			
	9	6	4	8	7		
	2	7	5	3	1	4	6
	6	8	9	2	4	5	7
	1	3	2		5	8	9